WORLD OF

WITCHES & WIZARDS

Paul Dowswell

Consultant: Susan Greenwood

southwater

This edition is published by Southwater

Southwater is an imprint of Anness Publishing Ltd
Hermes House, 88–89 Blackfriars Road, London SE1
8HA
tel. 020 7401 2077; fax 020 7633 9499
info@anness.com

© Anness Publishing Ltd 2001, 2002

Published in the USA by Southwater, Anness
Publishing Inc.; fax 212 807 6813

This edition distributed in the UK by The Manning
Partnership; tel. 01225 852 727; fax 01225 852 852;
sales@manning-partnership.co.uk

This edition distributed in the USA by National Book
Network; tel. 301 459 3366; fax 301 459 1705;
www.nbnbooks.com

This edition distributed in Canada by General
Publishing ; tel. 416 445 3333; fax 416 445 5991;
www.genpub.com

This edition distributed in Australia by Sandstone
Publishing ; tel. 02 9560 7888; fax 02 9560 7488;
sales@sandstonepublishing.com.au

This edition distributed in New Zealand by The Five
Mile Press (NZ) Ltd; tel. (09) 444 4144; fax (09) 444
4518; fivemilenz@clear.net.nz

A CIP catalogue record for this book is available from
the British Library

Publisher: Joanna Lorenz
Managing Editor, Children's Books: Gilly Cameron
Cooper
Editors: Lisa Miles, Louisa Somerville
Editorial Reader: Richard McGinlay
Series Design: John Jamieson
Designer: Margaret Sadler
Illustration: Peter Bull, Vanessa Card, Chris Forsey,
  Terry Gabbey, Guy Smith, Clive Spong
Picture Research: Veneta Bullen
Photography: John Freeman
Stylist: Melanie Williams
Production Controller: Don Campaniello

Anness Publishing would like to thank the following
children, and their parents, for modelling for this book:
Harriet Bartholomew, Alex Martin-Simons, Adrianne
Punzalan, Ben Rodden

PICTURE CREDITS - b=bottom, t=top, c=centre, l=left,
r=right

AKG Photo: 5tl, 5bl, 8br, 8bl, 9tr, 9cl, 9bl, 11tr, 12br,
26br, 26bl, 31bl, 31tl, 34bl, 37br, 37tr; E.T Archive:
5br, 5b, 7tr, 10bl, 23tl, 23tr, 23bl, 30tr, 31tr, 31ct, 37tl,
45cl; 53tl; Bridgeman Art Library: 4br, 6b, 9cr, 13tl,
30bl, 44br; Dover publications: 5tr, 27tl, 27bl, 39c,
39bl, 52tl; Mary Evans Picture Library: 4bl, 12bl, 13tr,
15b, 15tr, 16bl, 19tl, 22bl, 22br, 23br, 23c, 38bl, 38br,
44bl, 45t, 52bl, 52br, 53br, 53tr, 53bl, 58br, 58bl;
Fortean Picture Library: 7tl, 15tl, 18bl, 27c, 31br, 36br,
36bl, 48bl, 49tl, 59tr, 59cl, 59bl; Werner Forman
Archive: 51tr; Ronald Grant Archive: 4tr, 54bl, 55tr,
55tl, 55bl, 5cr; The Kobal Collection: 54br; Peter
Newark's Historical Pictures: 13bl, 18br, 39tr, 42bl,
43tr, 43tl, 43br, 45b, 48tl, 49tr, 48br, 49c; Eye
Ubiquitous: 49br.

Printed and bound in China

10 9 8 7 6 5 4 3 2 1

CONTENTS

Witches and Wizards

Did witches and wizards ever really exist? Are they still around today? The answer to both questions is yes. Throughout history in every society, certain people have practiced magic. That is, they have tried to make something good or bad happen by using spells and supernatural forces. We call these people witches, a word that often describes women who practice magic. Male witches may be called wizards or warlocks. Witches and wizards may also be called sorcerers, magicians, witch doctors, or shamans, depending on the time and place that they came from. In many cultures today, magic is a thriving and valuable part of everyday life.

Some of the ideas we have about magic are based on fact, or on legend, but many are complete inventions. In Europe, in the period between 1450 and 1650, people were obsessed by witch-hunting, an obsession created by the Christian church. Thousands of innocent people were arrested as witches, and then tortured, and executed. Some truly believed they had magic powers, but others were tortured into admitting things they did not do. This is the era from which many traditional images of witchcraft come.

▲ A PRIME SUSPECT
Any poor old woman living alone with just animals for company would have been a prime suspect for being labeled a witch in Early Modern Europe. Many villagers and townsfolk were convinced that witches made evil magic (called black magic) in their community. Even harmless village wisewomen, who told fortunes or made healing concoctions and love potions, were suspected of being witches. Although some of those accused may have been practicing black magic, most suspects were completely harmless, and some may even have been mentally ill.

▲ ENCHANTING SORCERESS
Witches from myths and legends were not all sharp-faced old hags. Some were beautiful and beguiling young women, such as Morgan le Fay, seen here dressed in sumptuous silks and velvets, casting a magic spell. Morgan was a sorceress and the enemy of the legendary King Arthur of Britain, who was supposed to have ruled around A.D. 450. Like many witches from all times and cultures, Morgan was supposed to have had the power to fly.

◄ HUBBLE BUBBLE
Witches gather around a bubbling cauldron in the company of demons, to brew up an evil spell. This is how it was imagined that witches behaved. People suspected of being witches were once put to death in Europe. The photograph comes from the Swedish film, Witchcraft Through the Ages. It was made in 1922, and is still frightening today. It is a silent horror movie that supposedly tells the story of witchcraft.

▼ MAGIC AND SCIENCE

From the 1500s, people called alchemists made half-magical and half-scientific experiments in an attempt to discover the legendary philosopher's stone. This was a substance that would enable them to turn ordinary metals into gold and guarantee eternal life. Alchemy was the forerunner of early chemical discoveries.

▶ NORTH AMERICAN SHAMAN

Clothed in wolfskin, this shaman is from the North American Blackfoot tribe. Holding a spear and a tambourine to assist his magic, he performs an elaborate ritual dance that will lead a dying man safely into the spirit world. Shamans and magical healers were important members of their communities. They cured the sick with specially chosen herbs, performed rituals and dances—often in a trance-like state, chanted, and said prayers that would bring good fortune to their people.

▼ JOIN THE CLUB

Witches gather together for a sabbat. This was a ceremony in which the Devil was supposed to be summoned and evil magic was done. The picture is entitled Witches' Kitchen and was painted by Hieronymus Francken, who lived from 1540 to 1610. At this time in Europe, fear of witchcraft was at its height. The women here are surrounded by ghoulish objects—a severed head, skulls, daggers, spell books, and odd creatures.

▼ CONJURING UP MAGIC

A wizard summons magical forces to help him in his work. As he follows a complicated spell through to its climax, a ball of light containing magical letters appears before him. Men were called witches, as well as wizards and warlocks. These are male magicians or sorcerers who are supposed to have magic powers.

World of Magic

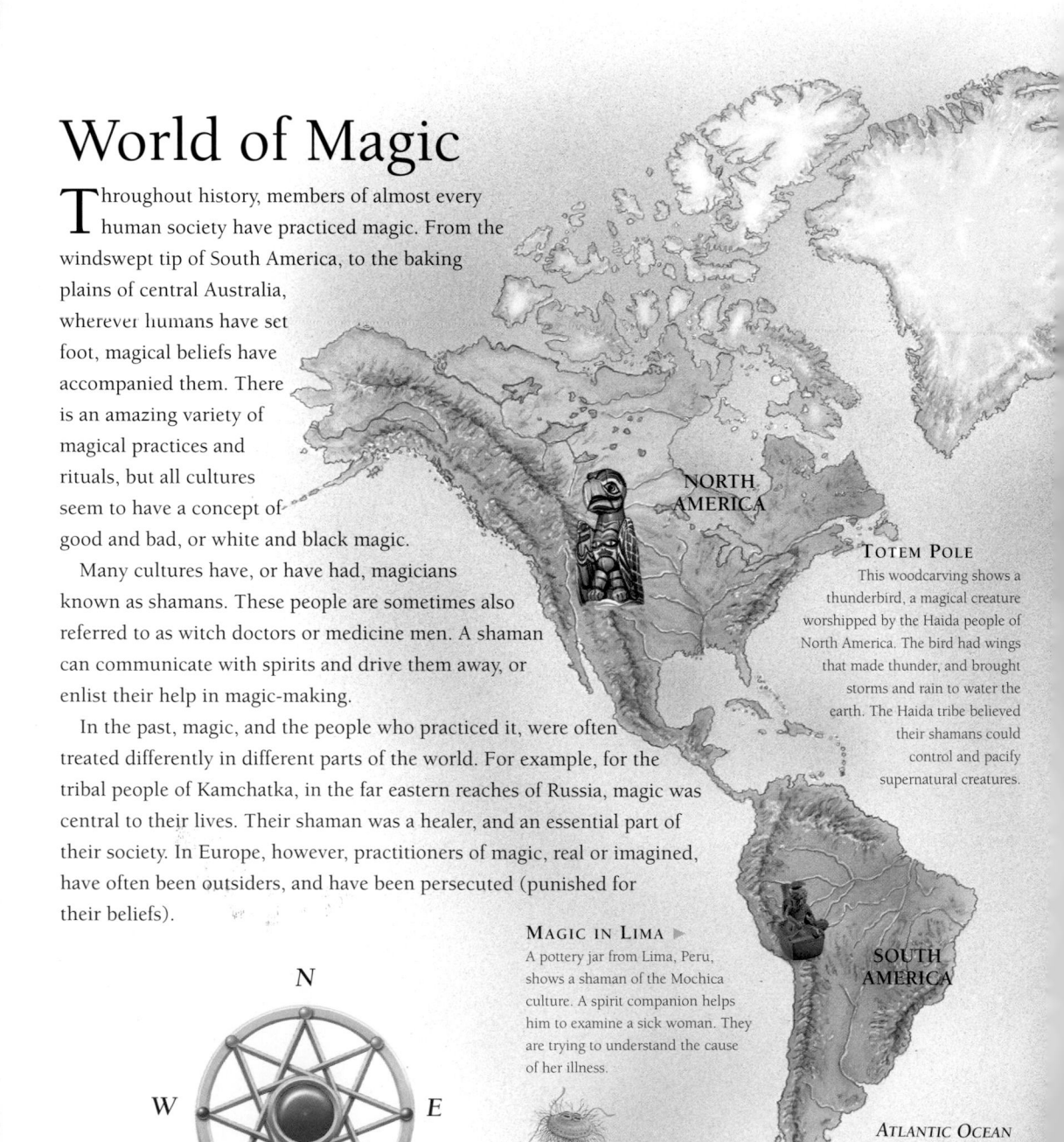

Throughout history, members of almost every human society have practiced magic. From the windswept tip of South America, to the baking plains of central Australia, wherever humans have set foot, magical beliefs have accompanied them. There is an amazing variety of magical practices and rituals, but all cultures seem to have a concept of good and bad, or white and black magic.

Many cultures have, or have had, magicians known as shamans. These people are sometimes also referred to as witch doctors or medicine men. A shaman can communicate with spirits and drive them away, or enlist their help in magic-making.

In the past, magic, and the people who practiced it, were often treated differently in different parts of the world. For example, for the tribal people of Kamchatka, in the far eastern reaches of Russia, magic was central to their lives. Their shaman was a healer, and an essential part of their society. In Europe, however, practitioners of magic, real or imagined, have often been outsiders, and have been persecuted (punished for their beliefs).

NORTH AMERICA

TOTEM POLE
This woodcarving shows a thunderbird, a magical creature worshipped by the Haida people of North America. The bird had wings that made thunder, and brought storms and rain to water the earth. The Haida tribe believed their shamans could control and pacify supernatural creatures.

MAGIC IN LIMA ▶
A pottery jar from Lima, Peru, shows a shaman of the Mochica culture. A spirit companion helps him to examine a sick woman. They are trying to understand the cause of her illness.

SOUTH AMERICA

ATLANTIC OCEAN

N

W E

S

EUROPEAN DRUIDS
Druidism was the religion of the Celtic peoples of the pre-Christian British Isles and Gaul (present-day France). The Druids regarded the oak tree as sacred. One of their chief rituals was cutting mistletoe from the oak tree with a golden sickle. They believed in reincarnation, were experts in astronomy, and may have offered human sacrifices.

▼ EASTERN SHAMAN
Dressed in animal hide robes, and carrying his ceremonial drum, a shaman from Kamchatka, in far eastern Russia, performs a magic ritual. Magic workers all over the world make use of music, rhythm, and dance.

RUSSIA

EUROPE

ASIA

AFRICA

PACIFIC OCEAN

INDIAN OCEAN

AUSTRALIA

ABORIGINAL MAGIC ▶
The body of this Australian Aborigine is covered with the magical markings that identify him as a tribal medicine man. Like shamans all over the world, his society believes he can communicate with spirits, who help him work his magic.

AFRICAN MEDICINE MAN ▲
In many parts of Africa, belief in the power of the magician to heal the sick is still common today. The man in this picture is a South African medicine man. He is probably in a trance, and seeking out spirit helpers to aid him in his work.

In Ancient Times

From the start of human history, people have believed in the power to influence people and events by the use of supernatural forces. In Stone Age cave paintings of bison and horses more than 15,000 years old, there are also drawings of strange, semihuman figures. Some archaeologists think these are witch doctors or shamans performing magic rituals. Ancient Egyptians, Greeks, and Romans, too, all had beliefs and traditions that accepted magic as part of their everyday lives.

People may have feared sorcerers, because they knew they could practice both good and bad magic, but they also felt that they needed them. If they were sick or about to set out on a journey, magic spells and rituals were performed to please the gods and to ask for their protection. Over the centuries, the magic and myths of early civilizations were woven into European culture. People's ideas about witches were based on these ancient magicians and sorcerers, and on ideas put forward by the Christian Church during the witch-hunts of 1450–1650.

▼ STONE AGE MAGIC

Deep inside a cave, a Stone Age shaman, dressed in an antlered headdress, is leading a ritual to insure that there will be plenty of game to hunt in the year ahead. Shamans were thought to have a direct link to the gods. Their rituals were intended to insure that the community was in touch with the spirits.

◀ ANIMAL MAGIC

This ancient wall painting, half-man, half-animal, is called the Dancing Sorcerer. It was discovered in a cave at Les Trois Frères, in the French Pyrenees mountains. The figure has wolf's ears, stag's antlers, bear's paws, and a horse's tail, and it is believed to be a Stone Age shaman.

▶ EGYPTIAN BABOON GOD

Thoth, the ancient Egyptian god of the moon and wisdom, was believed to be the creator of art, science, and magic. Thoth is shown here as a baboon with a student at his feet. Like many magical creatures, he could change his appearance. He is often shown as a man with the head of an ibis (a large bird). Shape-changing gods appear in several ancient myths, and this ability was also attributed to witches.

◀ CIRCE AND HER PETS

According to legend, the wild animals that surrounded the ancient Greek sorceress, Circe, were once men. Circe transformed them using a magic potion. The idea that witches could turn themselves and others into animals, and that they kept particular animals as servants, has its roots in the myths of ancient Greece and Rome.

▶ HORNED GOD

This human-like image of Cernunnos, the Celtic deer god, was engraved on a silver cauldron around 100 B.C. Often, the god is shown surrounded by animals, which suggests that he has special powers over them. Like the Greek god Pan, Cernunnos had horns. These horns made a reappearance in Christian images of the Devil, whom witches were said to worship and obey.

◀ BLOOD AND GUTS

On the opposite side of this Greek bronze mirror is etched Chalenas the soothsayer (fortune-teller). Soothsayers, both male and female, were able to predict future events by various methods, such as the examination of the internal organs of sacrificed animals. The Greeks and Romans were firm believers in the ability to see into the future. Palm reading and astrology were both popular in ancient Rome. Some soothsayers used unusual techniques, such as reading the movements of clouds and birds.

◀ FUTURE TRANCE

In ancient Greece, an oracle was a holy place where people could go to ask the advice of the gods through a human interpreter. This scene takes place at the site of the most famous oracle in history, the shrine of the god Apollo, in Delphi. His interpreter is a priestess called the Pythia. She sits on a huge tripod and chews laurel leaves. These contain a drug that sends her into a trance, during which time she communicates with Apollo. The priestess then predicts the fate of the questioners. The ability to see into the future has been a talent of magicians throughout history.

◀ WILD TIMES

Half-dressed men and women, wild with excitement, dance in a frenzy around Bacchus (called Dionysus in ancient Greece). He was the god of wine and intoxicating herbs, and plants such as ivy and laurel. In ancient Greece and Rome, Bacchus and other gods of pleasure and indulgence, such as Pan, were worshipped in mysterious cult ceremonies. They involved wild drinking, dancing, and the sacrifice of animals. How people imagined sabbats (witches' gatherings) was directly inspired by ancient rituals such as these. At sabbats, though, it was the devil who was center of attention.

Good Luck Charm

An amulet is a magic charm that people wear or carry to protect them against evil spells. They have been worn since ancient times, and they are supposed to bring good luck to the wearer. The amulet in this project is based on an ancient Egyptian design. It features a symbol called an udjat, which represents the eye of the sky god Horus. Amulets of this type became especially popular around 1000 B.C. A gold amulet would only have been worn by the Pharaohs (kings) of Egypt, since gold was thought to be the flesh of the sun. This privilege was later extended to priests and nobles.

You will need: felt-tipped pen, ruler, corrugated cardboard, scissors, masking tape, a few teaspoons of plain flour, water for mixing, mixing bowl, metal spoon, newspaper, chopping board, fine sandpaper, sheet of paper, fine paintbrushes, bright blue, dark blue, gold, black, and white acrylic paints, pencil, colored tinfoil candy wrappers, glue, glue brush.

A bright blue stone has been carved into the shape of a scarab beetle and polished to make an amulet (magic charm). It is from ancient Egypt and more than 3,000 years old. Amulets were placed on the chest of an embalmed corpse (preserved with oils and spices) to represent the heart. A dead person's heart was removed and embalmed separately. The amulets were believed to protect dead people in the next world. The scarab beetle represented the sky god, Horus, and was sacred to the Egyptians. The base of this amulet is covered in hieroglyphs (Egyptian writing). On either side are udjat eye symbols. Udjat means healing or protection, and symbolizes the god Horus's eye, which was torn out by his murderous uncle, Seth. Thousands of udjat amulets have been found wrapped up in Egyptian mummies.

1 Use a ruler to measure out and draw a rectangle on the piece of corrugated cardboard. The rectangle should measure about 9 ¼ x 2 ½ inches.

2 This is for the basic bracelet shape. Cut neatly around the edges of the rectangle you have drawn, using the pair of scissors.

6 Leave the amulet to dry completely. Then gently rub it with fine sandpaper to smooth the surfaces. Place a sheet of paper underneath to catch the flakes.

7 Paint the amulet all over in a bright color, such as light blue. It is better to use acrylic paint, because it is slightly water-resistant and will not smear.

10 Cut some bright-colored tinfoil candy wrappers into ¼-inch strips. Snip each strip across to make lots of ¼-inch squares.

11 Using glue and a fine glue brush, carefully glue the tinfoil squares around the top and bottom borders of the amulet. Leave to dry completely.

12 Use a fine paintbrush and gold, dark blue, black, and white paints to color in the pencil design on the amulet. Leave to dry.

13 Use more gold paint to decorate the inside of your amulet. Make sure the paint is completely dry before you wear the amulet.

8 When the paint is dry, use a pencil to draw a design on it. You could copy the eye of Horus, as shown here, or make up your own Egyptian-theme design.

9 Continue your pattern all the way around your amulet. For the border design, draw lines around the top and bottom of the amulet ½ inch from the edges.

Your finished amulet makes an attractive piece of jewelry. In Egyptian times, the amulet would have been made of precious stones such as lapis lazuli set in solid gold and worn by a king or a noble. It would have brought health and good luck.

This is the top and bottom of a heart-shaped scarab amulet, which is also around 3,000 years old. The writing on the underside asks the amulet (which represents the dead person's heart) not to say bad things against its owner when he is judged by the gods in the afterlife.

3 Bend the card around to form a bracelet shape. (You could try it on now to make sure it fits.) Overlap the edges slightly, and fasten them with masking tape.

4 Put some flour in a bowl. Slowly add water, stirring as you go, until you have made a thick paste. Then tear up strips of newspaper.

5 Now work on a chopping board. Dip strips of the newspaper into the paste. Cover the amulet inside and out with about 3 layers of papier-mâché.

Medieval Magic

In pre-Christian Europe, most people believed in not just one god, but many gods. Christianity and the teachings of Jesus spread throughout the Roman Empire, and in A.D. 313 became the official religion. This brought major changes to everyday life. In A.D. 476, the Empire fell when western Europe was overrun by the Visigoths, barbarian tribes from Germany. Europe entered an unsettled 600-year period that is often called the Dark Ages. During this time, the Christian Church was about the only unchanging element in peoples' lives.

People still believed that some men and women could cure disease and make love potions. However, they also feared that the same individuals had darker powers, such as causing crops to fail, or bringing illness and death upon their enemies. In the Middle Ages (1050–1450), the Church wanted to stamp out such beliefs. They were called heretical because they did not fit in with the Church's teachings.

▶ A DEAL WITH THE DEVIL

The Greek monk, Theophilus, is about to accept a written contract, or pact, which is being forced on him by a fearsome-looking Devil. According to legend, Theophilus, with the help of a sorcerer, sold his soul to the Devil during the A.D. 500s. He then had second thoughts and was eventually able to regain his soul. This tale became the inspiration for one of the most famous pacts in literary history. The plot was used as the basis for Dr. Faustus, a play by Elizabethan dramatist Christopher Marlowe. In the play, a scholar sells his soul to the Devil in exchange for supernatural powers and eternal youth. As witchcraft hysteria took hold of Europe, the story became mixed with other myths, and people suspected all witches of making a similar pact.

▶ MEPHISTOPHELES

Thirteen centuries after the original tale, the myth of selling souls to the Devil was still worth telling. This illustration from the 1800s shows Dr. Faustus with Mephistopheles, who was sent by the Devil to be Faustus' servant. Marlowe's play Dr. Faustus is still performed today.

▶ SATANIC ARISTOCRAT

One of the most notorious sorcerers of the Middle Ages was the Frenchman Gilles de Rais. Born into an aristocratic family in 1404, he was reputed to live more lavishly than the king. Seeking new ways to finance his luxurious lifestyle, he dabbled in alchemy, in the hope of turning ordinary metals into gold. He also developed an interest in Devil worship, and intended to persuade the Devil to help him gain greater wealth and power. He was reported to have kidnapped and killed 140 children for black magic rituals.

GOD AND MAGIC ▶

Albertus Magnus (1193–1280) was the bishop of
Ratisbon in Germany and a student of magic,
alchemy, and philosophy. At that time, monasteries
and cathedrals were great centers of learning, and
churchmen were some of the most educated and
open-minded men of their day. Many were
interested in investigating all that
science, magic, and religion had to
offer. Before hysteria about witchcraft
took hold in Europe, many churchmen
saw nothing wrong with the study and
even the practice of magic.

◀ JEALOUS WITCHCRAFT

King Henry II of England kept his
beautiful mistress, Rosamund, hidden
in a secret room in one of his houses.
During his rule (1154–1189), he banned anyone from his court who
practiced magic. However, it was rumored that his wife, Queen Eleanor, was
a witch. She found out about Rosamund and was jealous of her. Eleanor
discovered where she was hiding by following a thread that led to her room.
Then she offered Rosamund a poisoned drink, which killed her.

◀ FRENCH HEROINE

The French heroine, Joan of
Arc, rides in front of her
followers, wearing white
armor. She is going to meet
the heir to the French throne,
later Charles VII. Joan was the
daughter of a poor farmer. At
the age of 16, she claimed to
have heard the voices of saints
and angels urging her to drive
the English out of France. She
persuaded King Charles to let
her command a force against
them. Her victories inspired
the French, but she was
captured and put on trial by
the English. They accused her
of heresy (opposing the beliefs
held by the Church). The
charges against her included
keeping company with devils.
She was burned at the stake at
Rouen in France, in 1431.

Early Witch Hunts

From 1450 to 1650, the fear of witches was widespread in Europe. Witches, real or imagined, were persecuted in what the Church saw as an out-and-out war between good and evil. The majority of the accused were unfortunate innocent people. Antiwitch hysteria was increased by publications such as the *Malleus Maleficarum* (Hammer of Witches) in 1486, and the *Compendium Maleficarum* (Handbook of Witches) in 1626. These books set out rules for detecting witchcraft and were very prejudiced against women. The contents were based upon the imagination of the writers or the confessions of torture victims, and shaped people's views of how witches behaved.

Fierce religious struggles, as Protestants broke away from the Church in Rome, encouraged an obsession with witchcraft—witch hunts were used to get rid of opponents. From 1580, the number of trials rocketed.

▲ IMPRISONED!
Chained to a cold cell wall, with her hands tied above her head, a bewildered woman awaits her fate. The fear felt by those arrested and imprisoned for witchcraft can hardly be imagined. Unless they freely confessed to being a witch, suspects were often tortured until they did so. Courts were not allowed to pass a sentence without such a confession, but anyone successfully convicted of witchcraft faced execution.

▲ HOMAGE TO SATAN
Sitting on an ornate wooden throne, in an isolated countryside location, the Devil instructs witches in the secret art of black magic. It is not just women who have come to listen; several of those gathered before him are men. The way the Devil is depicted—a horned goat's head on the body of a man, scaly bat wings and taloned feet—is typical of the time. This illustration and the one below are from *Compendium Maleficarum*.

► REJECTING GOD
Witches and wizards line up to pay their respects to the Devil. They trample on the cross, the most sacred symbol of Christianity. People believed that witches conducted ceremonies that mocked the Christian religion. This was at a time when Protestants were rebelling against the rule of the Catholic Church in Rome. The Church authorities often accused people who did not go along with their ideas, of witchcraft.

▲ EVIL TRICKS
Demonic creatures circle in the sky above, while the Devil instructs four old women in the dark art of making wax images, or hex dolls. People believed that not only did witches ally themselves with the Devil, but they were also taught the black arts by him. This woodcut from around 1680 shows a widely believed aspect of witchcraft—that wax or wooden images of a person were made so that evil magic could be worked upon them. It was thought that if the doll was deformed or destroyed, then injury or death would befall the person it resembled.

► BROUGHT BACK FROM THE DEAD

The magician Edward Kelly summons a corpse from the grave in Lancashire, England. In many cultures, witches and wizards are said to be able to raise the dead, and European witches were no exception. Kelly was a friend of Queen Elizabeth I's royal astronomer, Dr. John Dee. Kelly liked people to believe that he was an alchemist and that he had other magical powers, too. If a scene such as the one shown here ever took place, it was no doubt performed with a great deal of trickery.

▲ UP BEFORE THE KING

James I, who ruled England and Scotland from 1603 to 1625, showed no mercy toward people condemned of witchcraft. He was fascinated by the supernatural and wrote a book called *Demonology*. It was an account full of extraordinary stories based on not much more than gossip, rumor, and confessions that were extracted through torture. James wrote it following an alleged attempt on his life by a group of men and women called the North Berwick witches. These are the people who are shown cowering before him in the picture.

◄ TAKING TO THE SKIES

A gaggle of witches, with black robes and pointed hats, circles an isolated country church. This engraving is taken from *Letters on Demonology and Witchcraft* by the Victorian writer Sir Walter Scott. It was used to illustrate a story about the North Berwick witches. Deserted graveyards were supposed to be witches' favorite location for casting spells.

Dress like a Witch

T This project will show you how to create the familiar image of a witch, dressed in ragged clothes with a broomstick. You could also make up a wrinkly, warty face and black teeth. This appearance developed from a feared figure from folklore—the hag. Myths and legends, from ancient Egypt to pre-Christian Europe, concern ugly old women, who were said to use demonic powers to bring misfortune to those around them. Unfortunately, in the days of witch persecution, many poor, old women looked like the hags of folklore and became the obvious targets for witch hunts.

You will need: pencil, ruler, scrap paper, black cotton fabric 2 ¼ yards × 45-inch, white pencil, scissors, needle, sewing thread, newspaper, stiff paintbrush, silver paint, A2 sheet of thin black card, Scotch tape, black card 12 x 12 inches, silver card, glue, glue brush, green and black tissue paper.

This fairy-tale illustration from the 1800s, by Kate Greenaway, has all the classic features we have come to expect in a witch. She hovers before us, broomstick in hand, her shabby cloak billowing in the light of the full moon.

1 Using a pencil and ruler, copy the above template onto some scrap paper, such as a piece of old newspaper.

45 in

30 in

18 in

40 in

12 in

6 Lay the dress on newspaper. Dip the brush in silver paint. Pull the bristles back toward you to spray paint onto the fabric. When dry, spray the other side.

7 Roll a piece of thin, black large card into a cone shape. Use a white pencil to draw a line on the card to show where it overlaps and should be taped.

11 Cut around the outside of the ring. Cut out the middle, leaving an extra 1 ¼ in inside the ring. Make snips into the ring, up to the inner line.

12 Fit the hat rim onto the bottom of the hat. Use Scotch tape to stick the tabs that you snipped in the rim to the inside of the hat.

2 Fold the black fabric in half longways. Lay it out on a flat surface. Use the template to draw the witch's dress shape onto the fabric with a white pencil.

3 Cut out the dress shape. Cut a slit 9 ½ in across the middle of the folded edge, for your neck. Cut a second line 4 ¾ in long down the back of the fabric.

4 Turn the fabric inside out. Using a needle and thread, sew a simple running stitch up each side and under the arms of the witch's dress.

5 Snip a jagged edge along the cuffs of each sleeve and along the bottom of the dress. Turn the dress inside out (so that the fabric is right side out).

8 Trim the excess card. Roll the card back into a cone shape and tape with Scotch tape. Trim the bottom edge of the cone to fit your head.

9 Place the hat on a piece of black card about 12 inches square. Using a white pencil, measure and draw a circle around the hat rim, but 2 in away from it.

10 Use a white pencil to draw a second circle around the hat, this time close to the rim. You should now have a ring 2 in wide.

Complete your witchy look with face paints. Paint dark lines under your eyes and around your mouth to make it look like you have wrinkles. You could also color one of your teeth with black lip liner. You will also need a broom, which you can make by tying twigs to an old broom handle or a long piece of thick dowel.

13 Draw a rectangular shape for a hat buckle onto silver card. Draw a second rectangle inside the first one. Cut out the buckle and glue it.

14 Cut green and black tissue paper into long strips for the witch's hair. Glue the strips to the inside of the hat, except at the front.

Animal Allies

T he eerie hooting of owls, cats screeching, toads croaking in the darkness of night—are all the noises what they seem, or could they be something more sinister? For many people who lived in Europe around the 1600s, animal sounds floating through the night air made them think that evil lurked outside their doors.

Some animals, particularly cats, toads, and owls, were believed to be associated with witches and wizards, and were called familiars. They were said by the Christian church to be demons who had taken animal shapes and assisted witches and wizards in their work. The reward for an animal's services was blood, either as a pinprick drop from the owner's finger, or taken from a sacrificed animal.

Familiars apparently could make themselves invisible and change from one animal into another. When a witch was accused and imprisoned, she would be secretly watched. If any animal came near her, even a fly, this would be used as proof that she was a witch receiving her familiars.

Witch's cauldrons traditionally contained a toad, a creature that people believed witches often changed into. People spat or threw a stone if they saw a toad, to avoid bad luck.

▶ FELINE ACCOMPLICE

Cats, particularly black ones, were thought to be the most common witches' companions. They were said to bring gifts such as flocks of sheep, or perform evil deeds such as murder, for their human owners. Cat familiars were given eerie names—Pyewacket, Grizel, and Prickeare are mentioned in accounts of witch trials. They were usually caught and tried along with their mistresses, and invariably met the same grisly fate. Fears that all cats were familiars sometimes led to total cat massacres in Early Modern towns or villages.

▼ OWL COMPANIONS

This elaborate engraving from the 1800s shows a witch preparing a spell. Her owl familiar hovers above—keeping watch, no doubt, for any meddling intruders. The owls huge, staring eyes, sinister hoot, eerily silent flight, and nighttime existence have long made it a creature associated with witchcraft. The Latin name for owl, strix, was the same word given to a witch.

▼ FLY GUYS

A witch stirs her magic brew, simmering in the cauldron, while her fly familiars watch. Many different kinds of animals were believed to be familiars. Ferrets, spiders, rabbits, and even hedgehogs were all cited in witchcraft trials.

▶ A SLIMY FRIEND

Toads are often mentioned as witches' companions. Their warty skin and love of damp hiding places has long made them seem sinister creatures to humans. In addition to helping a witch with her work, toads were also a handy source of ingredients for magic potions. A lotion made of toad spit, for example, was said to make a witch invisible. Witches were supposed to take great care of their familiars. The two toads in this illustration have been dressed in velvet capes with little bells, and taught to dance.

▶ GALLOWS MENAGERIE

This gruesome scene commemorates the hanging of the so-called Chelmsford witches. It appeared in a lurid pamphlet giving details of the case, published in 1589. It accused the women of "devilish practices and keeping of spirits"—a reference to the animals that supposedly helped them perform their witchcraft. In the foreground is one of the accused witches, Joan Prentice, who also hangs on the gallows behind. She is surrounded by several toads and a couple of monkeys. Her familiar stands on her lap to lick her face.

▶ A GIFT FROM SATAN

Satan, shown here in the middle, offers a familiar to a witch. The fierce-looking beast is unlike any real animal, but its sharp talons, long thick tail, and the heavy chain used to hold it, all suggest a creature of lethal power. This woodcut appeared in an English book called *The Kingdom of Darkness*. Published in 1688, it supposedly exposed the practice of witchcraft.

▶ WHAT'S IN THE POT?

A host of grotesque familiars attend a witches' sabbat. They gather around hopefully, as though they are expecting to be fed from the cauldron. This engraving depicts sinister goings-on in England in 1612. Like the strange black creature in the picture above right, many of these familiars are unlike any known animal. One has a dog's body and face, but human arms and legs. Another one has a bat's face and a dog's body.

Magical Decorations

Particular symbols and letters are said to have magical powers. You could use the shapes and symbols in these projects to make great decorations for a Halloween party. Either make a border around the room where you are holding the party, or hang them in the window. You could also make black silhouettes of cauldrons, broomsticks, and pointed witches' hats for your party decorations.

Halloween is celebrated on October 31st. It is an old European festival that marks the start of winter. Many present-day witches believe it is the time when communication with the dead is possible. The astrological symbols shown in the first project are associated with magic. Each symbol represents a particular sun sign. Astrology (the study of the planets and stars) is often used in an attempt to foretell the future, through the use of horoscopes. Black cats are often connected with witches, since they were believed to be familiars.

For the astrological symbol you will need: black card, ruler, plastic dish, white pencil, small pot, scissors, white and gold acrylic paint, paintbrush, glue, glue brush, tissue paper, tinsel string.

For the cat border you will need: sheet of black paper, ruler, scissors, white pencil, glue, glue brush, sheet of paper, glitter.

1 Take a piece of black card about 6 inches square. Place a slightly smaller dish on the card and draw around it with the white pencil.

2 Carefully place a smaller pot in the middle of the white circle. Draw around it. You will now have two white circles, one inside the other.

1 The template for the cat border is illustrated above. Cut out a piece of black paper about 10 x 40 inches. Fold the paper in half, then fold it in half again. Make sure the edges are creased firmly.

3 Using a white pencil, draw the cat shape onto the paper. The face, a front paw, a back paw, and the curl of the tail must touch the edge of the paper.

4 Carefully cut around the cat through the layers of paper. Be careful not to cut around the parts of the cat that are touching the edges.

5 Very carefully unfold the cat border. You should end up with four cats that are joined head to head, tail to tail, and paw to paw.

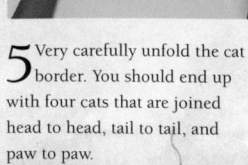

6 Lay the cat border down on your work surface. With a glue brush, dab a little glue where each cat's eyes should be, and on the tips of the paws.

3 Cut around the circles to make a hoop shape. Draw around the dish and pot again onto another piece of black card. Cut out a second hoop shape.

4 Decorate the hoops with sprinkles of gold and white paint. When they are dry, dab glue onto the back of one hoop. Stick it to a sheet of colored tissue paper.

5 Turn the tissue paper over. Fold a strip of black card in half and glue it to the top to make a loop to hang your symbol. Glue the second hoop in place.

6 Use scissors to trim the tissue around the edge of the hoop. Cut a sun sign from black card and glue it in the middle. Tie tinsel string to the loop.

2 Unfold the paper. Lay the paper flat with the short end toward you. Then fold the paper again, like a fan, along the creases.

SUN SIGNS

♑	Capricorn	♉	Taurus	♍	Virgo
♒	Aquarius	♊	Gemini	♎	Libra
♓	Pisces	♋	Cancer	♏	Scorpio
♈	Aries	♌	Leo	♐	Sagittarius

Your black cat border makes a wonderful decoration for any spooky party. You will need to make several borders in different colors to fit around the walls of a room. Use the same idea (a fan-fold and a large piece of paper) to make other border designs, such as owls and pumpkins.

7 Place a sheet of paper underneath the cats. Sprinkle glitter over the eyes and paws, and shake off the excess. Leave the cats to dry.

Magic Spells

"**E**ye of newt, and toe of frog; wool of bat, and tongue of dog; adder's fork, and blind-worm's sting; lizard's leg, and howlet's wing.**"**

These are some of the grisly ingredients that are listed in a spell recited by the three witches in the famous play *Macbeth*, by William Shakespeare. Spells were an essential part of a witch's work, and were spoken or written down in an attempt to influence people or events.

There were many different types of spells. Good ones promoted things such as healing, fertility, and long life. Bad ones caused illness, failure, and even death. Many spells had long been practiced by village wise men and women, who provided villagers with ancient remedies for illnesses and other afflictions. During the time when witches were persecuted, natural healers were no longer able to continue their work openly. However, spells from ancient times survive in the modern world as herbal remedies, in which the ingredients can have good effects on health.

▶ **HUMAN INGREDIENT**

Human remains have long been seen as a powerful ingredient in spells, as this ghoulish engraving from the 1800s shows. An English witch called Mother Chattox has ordered a servant to dig up a body. This will provide a gruesome ingredient for a spell that she plans to work on the hex doll that she carries. Fortunately for the local people, a good citizen lurking behind a tree has spotted her, and she will soon be punished. The account of this event is from 1612, so it is almost certainly a made-up story to spread bad feeling against witches.

▶ **RAISING A STORM**

Two witches prepare a spell around a boiling cauldron. While one adds a snake, the other plunges a cockerel into the bubbling water. They are making a spell to raise a storm, and in the sky above them, a seething mass of clouds spits hailstones. In Cornwall, England, people believed that witches were hired by smugglers or pirates to raise storms. The storms would drive ships onto the rocks, where their cargo could be stolen.

▶ **SECRET RECIPE**

Reaching down to pluck another ingredient for a spell, a witch hurries about her work under the cover of darkness. Many spells not only required the right plants, but also specified the time of day or night when they were to be picked. The moon has always had magical associations. Plants picked under the moonlight were thought to have special powers.

STORM IN A CAULDRON

A ragged witch dances on the edge of a cliff top beside a bubbling cauldron. She intends to drive a nearby ship to its destruction on the rocks. According to legend, witches could help seafarers, too. One spell sold to sailors enabled them to lock up the wind in a series of elaborate knots. When the ship had stabilized, the knots could be untied and the wind released.

LOVE POTION

Because it was frequently associated with romance and beauty, the rose was an ingredient in many love potions. Using techniques similar to those of perfume makers, witches would sometimes distil the rose oil in an effort to catch the essence of the flower's captivating qualities. Many spells were woven to entice a reluctant man or woman to fall in love. Plants such as the mandrake, periwinkle, and even salad leaves, such as endive lettuce, were also thought to be suitable ingredients for such spells.

A PRIZED POSSESSION

Strange, human-shaped mandrake roots have long been the most valuable ingredient in a witch's collection. Highly respected in many cultures because of its bizarre shape, mandrake is said to scream when it is picked. Although it is highly poisonous, mandrake was an extremely versatile ingredient, and was used as a sedative and an anaesthetic. Its initial effects promoted excitement, so it was mostly used in love potions. The mandrake root on the right was found in Denmark in the late 1800s—it resembles a skeletal man in a cloak. The fanciful drawing of the plant above is from a gardening manual from 1491.

HEART HEALER

Common foxgloves, with their purple, bell-shaped flowers, were often used in healing magic. Before the arrival of modern medicine, it was believed that herbal potions worked by magic rather than by science. Making healing spells was a very skilled art. If it is taken in large quantities, the leaves of a foxglove are poisonous and can easily kill a person. Used in small doses, however, the poison in them is an effective medicine for heart disease. A drug derived from foxglove leaves is still used today for patients with heart trouble. It increases the strength of heart contractions, and is used to regulate the heartbeat.

Make a Charm Bag

To cast a spell is to make a particular kind of magic for a specific purpose. All spells require a specific ritual with a series of actions that have to be performed in a certain way and at a chosen time. They also require ingredients, such as plants, stones, feathers, or soil.

A charm bag can be used to store a magical spell or to put crystals and other precious things in. This charm bag can be filled in a variety of ways. To help you to sleep well, put a little amethyst in the bag with a few sprigs of peppermint or some dried peppermint leaves. You could write a wish on a piece of paper. Fold it up and put it into the charm bag with some leaves from a willow tree. The willow tree is believed to help make your dreams come true.

You will need: dark blue velvet fabric, ruler, scissors, silver embroidery thread, large needle, pins, ordinary needle, dark blue thread, silver cord, crystals.

Put whichever crystal you feel you need into your pouch, and keep it under your pillow. For example, turquoise is for good luck, rutilated quartz is for happiness in love, and smoky quartz is for protection from bad atmospheres.

1 Take a large piece of dark blue velvet. Lay it flat, opposite side up. Use a ruler to measure a piece 12 x 9 inches and cut it out.

2 Take a piece of silver embroidery thread and thread it through a fairly large needle. Make a knot at the end of the thread.

5 Bring the needle through from the back of the fabric again, in the position shown. Push the needle back down into the fabric to create a cross.

6 Repeat these big stitches several more times to create a star, as shown. Finish at the back of the fabric. Cut the thread and tie a knot.

7 Sew more stars all along the bottom edge of the fabric. You could make them all the same size or make some smaller ones, too.

10 Fold the open end of the bag down. Fold it down again, so that there is no raw edge. Use pins to secure the edge.

11 Use the needle and blue thread to sew all around the edge of the bag. Use a running stitch again. Turn the bag the right way out.

12 Tie a knot in each end of a piece of silver cord. Sew the middle of the cord to the side of the bag, about 1 ½ inch down from the top.

13 Make sure the cord is sewn firmly to the side of the bag. Now put some crystals or lucky charms into your bag. Wrap the cord around to close it.

8 With the right side of the velvet up, fold the fabric in half widthwise. Pin together along the edge leaving the top edge opposite the stars open.

9 Thread an ordinary needle with blue thread. Knot the end of the thread. Sew along the bottom and the side of the bag, using a running stitch.

Crystals come in many different shapes and colors. They are magical objects that are said to be able to focus energy, and they are often used in healing rituals today. Fill your charm bag with crystals that you think are very beautiful.

3 Turn the velvet over, so it is right side up. Push the needle and thread through from the back of the fabric in one corner as shown.

4 Push the needle and thread back through the fabric about ½ inch diagonally away from where it came out. You have now made one large stitch.

Horseshoes are supposed to cast a protective spell over a house. They are made of iron, which is said to repel evil spirits. Supposedly, a horseshoe that is hung pointing downward will protect against witchcraft, and a horseshoe hung pointing upward will act as a good luck charm.

26

Secret Skills

The magical powers attributed to witches and wizards have a lot in common all over the world. According to myths and legends from many cultures, they can fly, shape-shift (change their shape) and make themselves invisible. So great was the fear of witchcraft, that many ordinary people invented the most extraordinary and ridiculous stories about witches.

Sorcerers and magicians also believed that they could do such things through their spells and potions. The sensation of flying, for example, could be achieved by taking mind-altering substances such as poisonous mushrooms. A witch might have stayed firmly on the ground, but in a trance, she would imagine herself to be spinning and weaving through the night sky at breathtaking speeds. Shape-shifting could also be explained in this way. Witches in a drug-induced state could imagine themselves being any animal they wanted. At first, the Church would not believe that witches could fly, become invisible, or turn into animals. Such actions were explained as illusions created by the Devil, instead of by authentic magic. Later, the Church saw witches as capable of all sorts of magical activities.

◀ HAGS INTO HARES

In Europe, witches were said to disguise themselves as hares, and run around stealing milk from cows, or spreading sickness to other farm animals. Stories were told of farmers who had trapped or shot at a hare, only to see it change back into an old hag before their eyes. This hare was drawn by Albrecht Dürer (1471–1528), a German artist of the period.

▶ FLYING BROOMSTICKS

These French illustrations from the 1400s are thought to be the first pictures of witches on their broomsticks. Why the idea of a witch on a broomstick became so popular is quite a mystery. Although the image became common in illustrations of witches around this time, the confessions used as evidence in witch trials rarely mention them.

▼ FADING AWAY

A witch fades into her surroundings after swallowing a magic potion to take on the cloak of invisibility. Spells found in books show that becoming invisible was a complicated business. One spell required seven black beans, a dead man's head, and an elaborate ritual to be followed over nine days. If the spell worked, the witch placed one of the beans in her mouth to become invisible. The instructions warn her not to swallow it, since taking the bean from her mouth was the only way to become visible again.

► LEARNING THE MAGIC

This Italian woodcut depicts a scene from *The Golden Ass* by the ancient Roman writer, Apuleius. While her servant Apuleius looks on, a witch begins to sprout feathers as she transforms herself into an owl. As she changes shape, she hides the magic ointment that has made this transformation possible in a cupboard. Apuleius watches from the other side of the door. He hopes to learn how the magic is done, but when he tries, he becomes an ass instead of an owl!

► FLYING SHAPE-SHIFTERS

Three shape-shifting witches take to the air as a hailstorm brews. One has a donkey's head, one has a chicken's head, and the other has a dog's head. This woodcut, taken from a German book published in 1489, may be the first illustration to show witches flying. It is unusual because it shows the witches riding a branch instead of a broomstick.

► FLY-FASTER OINTMENT

Broomstick in tow, a young witch gets ready to take to the night sky. Her accomplice, a ragged, pointed-faced old woman, is rubbing flying ointment over her body. Such ointments were supposed to be made from the fat of human babies, plus herbs and drugs. Mandrake root was linked with flying, probably because of its mind-altering effects.

► CAUGHT IN THE ACT

Unaware of a nosy neighbor watching them, four witches prepare to fly to a sabbat (a witches' gathering). It was believed that witches rubbed ointment in their bodies so that they could fly. Viewed from left to right in the picture, one prepares her broom, one applies flying ointment, one shoots up the chimney, and the last is already in the air. The illustration appears in a French book published in 1579.

A Witch Mobile

In the days of witch hunts, around 1450 to 1650, people really did believe that witches could fly. Many woodcuts and illustrated manuscripts from the period show them doing this. Sometimes they are carried by demons, sometimes they sit on branches, but most of the time they straddle brooms.

At certain times of the year such as Halloween, when witches were supposed to be out in numbers, church bells would be rung throughout the night. It was believed that the sound of the bells had the power to stop the witches from flying overhead.

Here you can make your very own mobile to show a group of witches flying through the night sky, heading for their lair.

1 Using the templates shown above, draw four witch bodies and eight arms on green card. Draw four hats freehand on black card.

You will need: pencil, thin green, black and white card, scissors, ruler, hay, four kebab sticks trimmed to 9 ½ inches, twine, glue, glue brush, eight pieces of black felt 6 x 6 inches, eight pieces of black felt 3 x 3 inches, black felt-tipped pen, gold and silver acrylic paint, paintbrush, two pieces of ¼-inch dowel 16 inches long, needle, sewing thread.

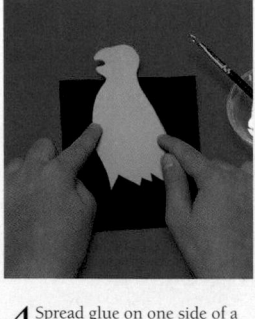

4 Spread glue on one side of a witch body (except the head). Press it onto a large square of black felt. Repeat with the other three bodies. Leave to dry.

5 Trim the felt around each witch body. Glue a broomstick across each witch body at an angle, as shown. Leave to dry.

6 Spread glue on the remaining green side (except the head) of a witch. Press onto another black felt square and trim. Repeat with the other three witches.

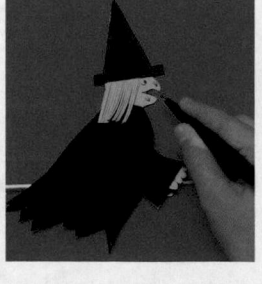

10 Glue two hat shapes on each witch's head. Using a black felt-tipped pen, draw details such as eyes, boils, and warts on each witch's face.

11 Paint the stars gold on each side, and paint the moon silver on each side. Paint the two pieces of thin dowel gold. Leave to dry.

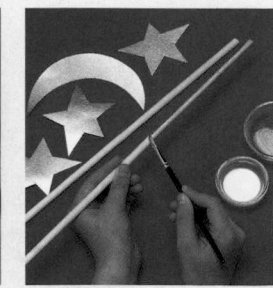

12 Cross the two pieces of dowel over at the center and secure them with twine. Leave a long piece of twine to hang the mobile up by and trim.

13 Thread a needle with thread and make a knot in the end. Pass the needle through the top of a hat, but not too near the top, or it may rip.

14 Trim the thread, leaving a long piece attached to the hat. Repeat for the other three. Tie the other end of the thread to the ends of the dowels.

15 Attach threads to the stars in the same way. Tie them between the witches and the middle of the mobile. Tie the moon to the center cross bar.

By hanging up the witches, stars, and moon at different heights, you will make your mobile more interesting to look at. Don't be scared if it starts moving in the middle of the night!

7 Glue each arm (but not the fingers) onto a small felt square. Make sure you glue one side of four of the arms, and the other side of the rest.

8 Leave the arms to dry. Then glue a pair of arms onto each witch. Leave to dry again. Now you are ready to make the witches' hair.

9 Cut two pieces of green card 2 x 1 inch. Make cuts into them lengthwise, leaving a ¼-inch strip at the end uncut. Glue in place. Repeat for each witch.

2 Carefully cut out all the witch bodies, arms, and hat shapes. Draw four stars and a crescent moon on the white card and cut them out, too.

3 Trim a small bunch of hay in to a bundle about 3 inches long. Tie the hay around the end of a kebab stick with twine. Repeat with three other sticks.

The Magic of Alchemy

Alchemy was an ancient art, half-magic and half-science. One of its major aims was to turn base (low value) common metals, such as copper, lead, zinc, and tin, into precious metals, such as silver and gold. No alchemist ever succeeded in doing this, but through their experiments they discovered a lot about the way materials react together. Their work was to lay the foundations of the modern science of chemistry. Alchemy first began in China and Egypt around 300 B.C. By the A.D. 700s, alchemical ideas had spread to the Middle East, and they reached Europe by the Middle Ages.

As part of their experiments, alchemists used spells and magical symbols to help them achieve their goals. They were deeply concerned for their souls, and their work had religious aspects. They had a motto, "*Ars totum requirit hominem*" (the art requires the whole man). It reflected their belief that through their work they could also perfect themselves as human beings.

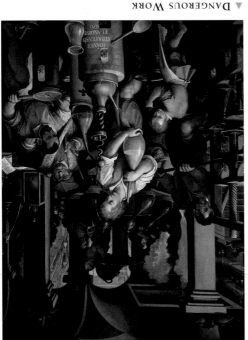

◀ DANGEROUS WORK

This Italian painting, by Giovanni Stradano, shows an alchemist's laboratory around 1570. The alchemist himself is seated to the right of the picture and is wearing a hat, a fur-lined coat, and glasses. His text book is open beside him, and he directs his assistants in their complex tasks. An alchemist's workshop must have been an extremely dangerous place to work, with its fragile pots and jars, open fires, and red-hot metals. After centuries of experimentation, alchemists never did succeed in changing base metal into silver or gold, but they did figure out how to make use of many chemicals.

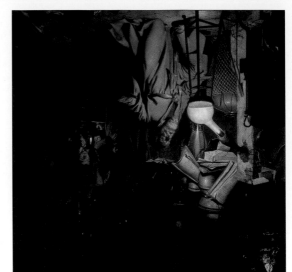

◀ GHOSTLY GLOW

The German alchemist, Hennig Brand, falls to his knees in wonder at the pale, luminous glow coming from inside a glass flask. Joseph Wright's painting of 1771 depicts Brand's workshop, bathed in the eerie light of burning phosphorus. Brand accidentally discovered this chemical in 1669, when he mixed together other substances. Many alchemists made vital discoveries such as this, and many of the pioneers of modern science took a deep interest in alchemy.

Paracelsus, which was first published in 1529.
illustration is taken from an alchemist text called *Practica* by
special properties that would be vital to their work. This
which is a liquid, silvery metal. They were convinced it had
element mercury. Alchemists were fascinated by mercury,
symbol Azoth, and it represents the essence of the
wings, and wriggling serpents' tails. It is the alchemist
and legs, a lion's mane, reptilian scaly skin, dragon
This bizarre creature is made up of a human head

▶ BIZARRE BEAST

substance that would give eternal youth.
searching for the elixir of life, a chemical
Alchemists were also preoccupied with
transform ordinary metals into pure gold.
philosopher's stone—a substance that would
alchemical process would produce the
combining these three elements in an
sulphur, and salt. It was believed that
symbolize the chemical elements mercury,
white birds inside a glass flask. The birds
book, *Splendor Solis*, shows black, red, and
An elaborate painting from the alchemist text

▶ THE PHILOSOPHER'S STONE

▶ SCIENTIFIC GENIUS

Sir Isaac Newton, who lived from 1642 to 1727, was probably the greatest scientist of his age. He made important discoveries in optics and motion that remain important in physics today. Like many learned men of his era, he took a great interest in alchemy. He followed alchemical experiments, and made reams of notes on the subject. He also contributed his own original ideas to alchemical theories on the makeup of different substances.

▶ MEDICAL PIONEER

One of the most famous alchemists was a Swiss physician called Paracelsus, who lived from 1493 to 1541. He was renowned as a medical pioneer. His innovations included using chemistry in medicine, the first clear descriptions of particular diseases, and an understanding of how immunization worked. He traveled widely in the Middle East, and searched for an undiscovered element that he believed could change base metal into gold and would be a cure-all medicine.

▶ ECCENTRIC PATRON

The eccentric Holy Roman Emperor, Rudolf II, was a great supporter of alchemy, especially in Prague in eastern Europe, where he kept his court. He also encouraged other scientists and astronomers in their work. He had a deep fascination for anything strange and unusual, and almost certainly suffered from some form of mental illness. In 1590, he commissioned the Italian artist, Giuseppe Archimboldo, to paint his portrait in the form of a collection of fruit and vegetables.

Magician at Work

Here you can see what a magician's workshop may have looked like in the early 1500s. This was an era of great excitement in Europe, called the Renaissance (meaning rebirth). New ideas about art, science, and medicine were becoming popular. The continents of North and South America had recently been reached by Europeans. For learned people, the world seemed to be brimming with new possibilities.

For some wealthy people, magic and alchemy were areas open to investigation, but both were forbidden arts. Those who practiced them risked being persecuted as heretics. A laboratory or workshop would have to be somewhere away from prying eyes, such as this basement below an ordinary shop in a town street.

By day, the magician runs a simple apothecary (drugstore) that sells herbs, spices, lotions, and potions to heal and help people. By night, and unknown to the townspeople, he practices his forbidden art and makes his spells, conjuring and creating by candlelight in the cellar of his shop.

◀ **MAGICAL MATERIALS**
The magician's assistant fetches more equipment and materials for a magical experiment. He has to be careful, because some of the ingredients are rare and fragile. The wizard is ready to create a spell. He wants to unlock the secrets of materials such as mercury, sulphur, salt, or even ordinary water. Maybe he will be able to turn them into something much more valuable, such as gold or precious jewels.

KEY
1 *magician*
2 *magician's assistant*
3 *astrological chart*
4 *telescope*
5 *crystal ball*
6 *pestle and mortar*
7 *apothecary's shop sign*
8 *stairs to shop*
9 *metal stirring rod*
10 *boiling flask*

▶ Burning Brew

The magician and his assistant are busy concocting their experiment. They are trying to turn iron into gold by melting, mixing, and burning different chemicals. By day, the customers in the shop upstairs sometimes wonder where all the heat is coming from. Little do they know about the fires that are burning below.

▼ Wondrous Works

The magician's world revolves around the study of strangely mysterious books. His motto is "*Obscurum per obscurius, ignotum per ignotius!*" (The obscure is to be explained by the more obscure, the unknown by the more unknown.) His books are packed with weird and wonderful symbols and illustrations. These big, leather-bound, gold-embossed volumes have been handwritten over the centuries by old masters of magical arts. The magician adds his own spells and formulas to one of the books. As he pauses for thought, he carefully inscribes the magical symbols of his craft, using a fine quill pen.

▼ New Worlds

The magician is intensely interested in the world around him, distant places, and the stars and planets beyond the Earth. He collects anything from foreign lands, especially from the newly discovered Americas. His pet monkey is his latest acquisition. It has been brought by ship from Central America.

Dress like a Wizard

Our image of wizards, like that of witches, is based on fairy tales and myths. Many stories concerning wizards date from medieval times, so their appearance is shaped by what people wore at that time. Wizards are also associated with alchemists who were often well-educated and rich members of society, which is why they are often pictured wearing sumptuous velvets and furs.

Wizards have never attracted the same hostility as witches. They are seen as mysterious magic workers, and as wise, rather than ugly and evil. This shows how women have been treated unfairly.

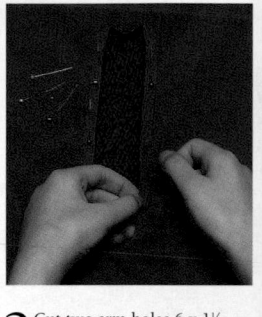

1 Cut a piece of red silky fabric measuring 64 x 52 inches. Pin the edges on the two short sides and one long side to make a hem. Then sew along the hem.

2 Cut two arm holes 6 x 1½ inches in the fabric 14 inches in from the shorter sides and 10 inches in from the unsewn edge. Pin around the arm hole edges.

You will need: scissors, ruler, red silky fabric, pins, needle, red sewing thread, red yarn, large safety pin, newspaper, silver fabric paint, fine paint brush, pencil, silver card, glue and brush, silver glitter, small safety pins, Scotch tape, pair of compasses or cup, ½-in dowel 14 inches long, red tissue paper, red card 24 x 24 inches, black felt-tipped pen, thin elastic.

7 Spread newspaper on your work surface, then lay the cloak over it. Use silver fabric paint and a fine brush to make swirls on the cloak, as shown.

8 To make a fastener for the cloak, draw a star shape on the silver card and cut it out. Glue glitter around the edges. Make three or four fasteners.

9 When the glue is dry, tape a small safety pin to the back of each fastener. When your cloak is on, pin them in place to hold the edges of it together.

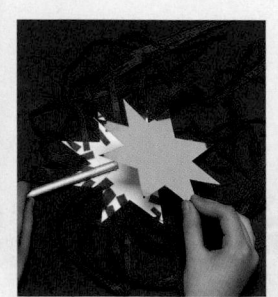

With his spell book in his hand, a wizard gets ready to make magic, clothed in flowing robes covered in mysterious symbols. Wizards always inspire fascination more than fear, and have usually been associated with good magic, rather than evil magic.

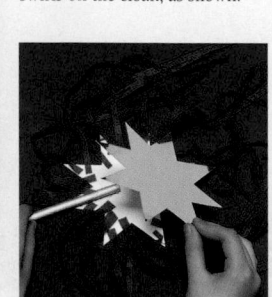

12 Now glue the second star onto the first star, on the same side as the dowel. Make sure that the points of the two stars are joined.

13 Roll the red card into a cone shape. Use a black felt-tipped pen to mark where it should be cut to get rid of the excess card. Unroll the cone.

14 Cut the card along the marked line. Roll up again and fasten with Scotch tape. Trim the bottom of the cone so that it will fit your head.

Wizards in myths and legends are often pictured as wise old men. Finish your wizardly wicked outfit with a long, white beard made of cotton or white styrofoam.

3 Make sure that the sides of the slits are pinned back on the same side of the fabric as the edges you have already sewn. Sew around the edges of the slits.

4 Fold the long unsewn edge of the fabric over about 1¼ inch deep. Pin the fabric into position, then sew. This makes a drawstring tube for the neck.

5 Cut 30 pieces of red yarn, each 56 inches long. Knot at one end. Divide the threads into bunches of ten and braid them. Tie a knot at the end of the braid.

6 Ask an adult to pin a large safety pin through one of the knots. Use the safety pin to pull the knotted braid all the way through the neck tube.

10 Draw a circle, 3¼ inches in diameter, on silver card. Use a compasse or draw around a cup. Draw triangles around it to make a star pattern. Cut out two stars.

11 Paint a piece of dowel silver. When it is dry, glue it to the back of one of the stars. Cut tissue paper into long, thin strips and glue them, too.

15 Decorate the hat to match your cloak, by painting it all over with silver swirls. Paint different types of swirls to make the design look more interesting.

16 Make a chin strap by making two small holes on each side of the hat using a pencil. Thread elastic through the holes and tie the ends.

Seeing the Future

S crying (forecasting the future) was a skill supposedly practiced by witches and wizards throughout the ages. Before the great witch hunts, a village wisewoman or man would have been consulted about the future. The term scrying comes from an old English word *descry*, which means "to make out dimly." This is a good description of how most tellings were performed. The scryer would stare into a blackened cauldron full of water, or a still pond on a moonlit night, and go into a trance. Fleeting, blurry images were said to appear. Sometimes they would be actual events, and sometimes they would be symbols that would need to be interpreted.

There were many ways of foretelling future events. The most common of all was astrology, a way of predicting the future via the movements of the stars and planets. Another way was palm reading, which involved interpreting the lines on the palms of a person's hands. How different playing cards fell or were dealt could also tell a person's future.

▲ A DARK REFLECTION

In the dead of night, a magician summons spirits to help him see into the future, with the aid of a vast, elaborate magic mirror. In addition to good souls waiting down from heaven, the magician also appears to have called up demons and damned souls from hell. It has always been believed that magic mirrors have magic powers, and that they could be used to see into the future. Dark mirrors, which are less reflective than ordinary mirrors, are supposed to be particularly effective.

▲ GLASS FUTURES

Crystal balls are still used for scrying to this day. The best crystals for scrying are said to be those made of semi-precious stone, such as beryl, a green or white mineral found in granite. Although crystal balls are frequently associated with fortune-telling, they were not commonly used in the past. They were heavy to carry around and expensive to buy. Witches who lived by the sea would use glass fishing floats, which were supposed to do the job just as well.

▲ INSIDE A CRYSTAL BALL

A witch peers into a crystal ball and an image is revealed to her. When she performed a fortune-telling, a scryer was thought to go into a trance. Images of future events that only she could see would appear from the swirling mist inside the crystal ball. Perhaps she would see a shipwreck, a marriage, or even a murder. Predicting the future was a very inexact art, and fortune-tellers needed a lot of practice to interpret their visions.

▼ LOOKING AHEAD

The witch Anne Bodenham is fortune-telling with the help of several demonic imps, a cat and dog familiar, and a magic circle drawn in the earth. This illustration is from Nathaniel Crouch's antiwitchcraft book, *The Kingdom of Darkness*, published in 1688. Bodenham stares into a seething cauldron of fire, her spell book in her hand. Behind her waits an accomplice, eager to see what the future holds.

◀ NOSTRADAMUS

The French physician Nostradamus, who lived from 1503 to 1566, is probably the most famous astrologer in history. He wrote two collections of prophesies called *Centuries*. His predictions, which were written in a series of rhymes, still attract a lot of interest today. Some people believe that Nostradamus predicted future events such as the rise and fall of Napoleon and Hitler, and the assassinations of President John F. Kennedy and his brother Robert. Others feel that his obscure, enigmatic verses can be interpreted in different ways. They can mean anything the reader wants them to mean.

◀ PALM READER

Telling the future from the lines on a person's hand is one of the oldest witchcraft skills. Palm reading in one form or another has been practiced in India and China since 3000 B.C. Like astrology, at one time it was considered to be a science. It was even tolerated by the Church. However, so many tricksters claimed they had the ability to read palms that the Church condemned the custom at the end of the 1400s. Even so, palm reading has remained a popular attraction at fairs and markets right up until the present day.

▼ CARDS OF FORTUNE

A Dutch painting from the 1500s shows a fortune-teller laying out cards in front of a customer. Each card has a meaning. For example, the two of hearts signifies new friendships, the two of diamonds means that trouble is brewing, and the ace of spades (the most feared card of all) signifies death. Using playing cards to see into the future was one of the most popular means of scrying.

The Sabbat

It was said by the Christian Church that at certain times of the year, groups of witches would leave their homes and meet in far away places. The tops of mountains, windswept moors, or deep in the darkest woods, were all likely venues far away from the prying eyes of ordinary folk.

Once they had gathered together, the witches would celebrate before their master, the Devil himself. These gatherings were called sabbats, a word based on sabbath, the Jewish and Christian holy day. It may be that the word sabbat came to be used because in Europe, during the Middle Ages, many people feared and disliked the Jews.

Sabbats were also supposed to include grotesque mockeries of the services of the Catholic Church. Reports of such gatherings inflamed (strengthened) antiwitch hysteria in Europe. Town dwellers and peasants alike listened with fascination and repulsion to tales of demonic conduct. Most historians, however, believe that the whole concept of the sabbat, like many other aspects of witchcraft, was invented by the Church in order to control heresy.

▲ DANCING IN THE DARK

On a windswept fall evening, witches and warlocks dance themselves into a frenzy around a blazing bonfire. It was believed that wild actions such as this were intended to create a suitable atmosphere for the Devil, the sabbat's principal guest, to appear. It was believed that child sacrifices, wild parties, and evil magic spells were performed at the sabbat, where no form of behavior was too outrageous. When the Devil did appear, he would scratch each attendant with his claw, making a mark on their skin. Any blemish on the skin was known to witch hunters as the Devil's Mark.

▲ DEVIL'S FOOD

Devils and witches feast together at a banquet during a sabbat. While they eat and talk, a host of devil servants brings freshly cooked food from two roaring bonfires. The food at sabbats tasted foul, according to accounts given at the witch trials. Salt was forbidden because witches hated salt, and rumors told that even babies were eaten on these occasions. This woodcut is from *Compendium Maleficarum* (*Handbook of Witches*).

ANCIENT ROOTS ▶

Witch-hunters may have gotten many of their ideas about sabbats from ancient myths and rites (rituals). Many ancient works of art show Greeks cavorting (dancing) with gods such as Dionysus and Pan, who were famous for wild parties. In this illustration, from around 1600, the dancers and demons are circling in a frenzy around a horned goat god. The goat is Satan, rather than the more playful, but mischievous Pan. Behind the revellers stands the silhouette of a gallows. This is a foreboding sign of the punishment to come when their demonic dabblings are finally discovered.

► WITCHES' PROPS

These are some of the props used to perform acts of evil magic. The severed hand has been hacked from the corpse of a hanged man. Called a Hand of Glory, it was used to hold candles, or it was burned as part of an ingredient in a spell. A sheep's heart studded with nails was another common prop. A hex doll would have been used to direct evil magic at a particular person.

◄ GARLANDS FOR THE DEVIL

Supposedly, the high point of any sabbat was the appearance of the Devil himself, most often in the guise of an animal. A goat was said to be Satan's favorite form, but sometimes the evil one would appear as a cat or even a toad. In this disturbing image by the renowned Spanish artist, Francisco Goya (1746–1828), the goat-devil has his horns garlanded with flowers. Around him, witches offer up starving children. Behind him, on the left, is a grotesque collection of hanging hex dolls, which were used to place curses upon victims. Goya was the court painter to the king of Spain. As he grew older, he spent more time creating scenes of fantasy and terror instead of portraits. At the time, Spain was occupied by France. Many of Goya's paintings reflected this difficult political situation.

◄ ► A PRETTY UGLY PAIR

These two bizarre creatures are supposed to be devils. The grisly looking creature with horns and long, taloned feet below is Belphegor. According to the Bible, Belphegor was an evil demon worshipped by the Moabites, enemies of the Israelites. The obese elephant-like demon is called Behemoth, and was a Biblical demon of animal strength. Demons were supposed to be fallen angels who became servants of the Devil. Their job was to tempt human beings away from God and into evil ways. Witches were said to meet with them regularly and entertain them at sabbats.

◄ THREE HEADS

A witch bows down to worship a bizarre three-headed demon. This illustration from 1544 shows that various witch stories became mixed-up in the telling, as they passed from one scaremonger to another. This demon seems to be a shape-shifter—a creature that can turn itself into different forms. However, instead of turning into just one half-animal shape, it has taken the heads of a lion, an eagle, and a snake—all of which have long been regarded as dangerous and powerful creatures.

Make a Jack-o'-lantern

Halloween, on October 31st, marks the old European festival of Samhain, which celebrated the start of winter, and was a time for remembering the dead. People celebrate Halloween for fun, and make eerie hollowed-out pumpkins for the occasion. The face on the pumpkin, with its hollow eyes and toothy grin, represents a lost soul. Such supernatural creatures have various names. They are called jack-o'-lanterns in the USA, will-o'-the-wisps in England, and foxfires in Ireland. It is said that they usually show themselves as glowing balls of light, which is why the pumpkin is lit from the inside. Here are two projects that show you how to make lanterns for an evening party.

For the jam jar lantern you will need: large jam jar, ruler, white pencil, thin black card, scissors, coloured tissue paper, glue, brush, Scotch tape, thin wire, wire-cutters, pliers, small candle.

For the pumpkin lantern you will need: a large and a small pumpkin, sharp knife, ice-cream scoop or large spoon, black felt-tipped pen, small candle.

1 Measure the height and circumference of the jam jar. Add ⅛ inch for overlap. Using a white pencil, draw a rectangular shape onto thin black card.

2 Cut out the shape. Use the white pencil to draw a pattern of diamonds on the rectangle. Very carefully, cut the diamonds out.

1 Take the pumpkin and ask an adult to cut a "lid" off the top with a sharp kitchen knife. Make sure that the top comes off in one piece.

2 Use an ice-cream scoop or a large spoon to remove and discard the insides of the pumpkin. You will need to scrape it very hard.

5 Look at your pumpkin's face to see if you need to add more features. You could cut out a nose or eyebrows, or some more crooked teeth.

6 Take the smaller pumpkin and ask an adult to cut off the top. Again, scoop out and discard the insides of the pumpkin.

Place a small candle inside the jar and ask an adult to light it for you with a match. Your jam-jar lantern will give out a dim, coloured glow.

3 Cut lots of different colored tissue into squares big enough to fit over the diamonds. Glue the tissue squares over the holes and leave them to dry.

4 When the glue is thoroughly dry, wrap the decorated paper around the jam jar, with the glued side facing inward. Seal the overlap with tape.

5 Cut some wire slightly longer than the neck of the jar. Twist the ends together. Cut some longer wire. Twist it around the first wire, as shown.

6 Loop the wire handle over the top of the jar. Ask an adult to help tighten the neck piece by twisting the wire with a pair of pliers.

3 Use a black, felt-tipped pen to draw a spooky face on the pumpkin. Draw triangles for the eyes. Draw a large grin with lots of pointed teeth.

4 Ask an adult to use a sharp knife to cut out the eyes and the mouth. Push the cut-out shapes inward, then pick them out and discard them.

Once you have made a traditional jack-o'-lantern with a crude face, you could also try using other patterns. Stars and curly lines make good shapes. The same as the jam-jar lantern, when your jack-o'-lantern is finished, place a candle inside it and ask an adult to light it for you with a match.

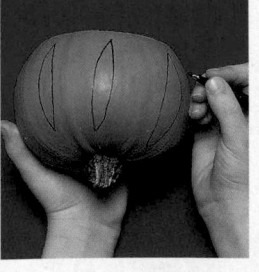

7 Using a black felt-tipped pen, draw a pattern of shapes onto the pumpkin to make a crown. Copy the shapes shown here, or make up your own.

8 Ask an adult to cut out the pattern. Put a small candle inside the large pumpkin, and then put the small pumpkin on top of the big one.

Witch-hunting

"Thou shalt not suffer a witch to live." So reads a passage in the Old Testament. Rarely has a verse in the Bible been so harshly used to justify such appalling cruelty. Over 250 years, from 1450 to 1700, hundreds of thousands of people were accused of witchcraft.

Nowhere in Europe was free of this persecution, which swept across the continent like a plague. It flared up in one country, then died down, only to burst out again in another. Anyone could be a suspect—priests and laymen, merchants and beggars, men and women—but most of all women. Although thousands of men were accused of witchcraft, it was almost always women who were burned at the stake or hanged from the gallows as punishment.

Some of those arrested probably practiced some form of magic, but most witch-hunt victims had nothing to do with witchcraft at all. Witch-hunting mania often erupted in a region following crop failure, disease, or war. The local population were desperate to vent their anger and frustration on anyone they could find. It was also used by the Christian Church for the control of heresy. However, most of those sent to their deaths were simply old, eccentric, or confused.

▼ WEIGHING A WITCH

To prove a suspect guilty, witch-hunters developed a series of bizarre tests. Weighing a witch was one of these tests. It was based on the logic that since witches could fly, they must be very light. The test varied from area to area. In some towns, a suspect would be weighed against a heavy Bible, or against a set weight that she had to equal. Either way, a guilty verdict was almost guaranteed. This image of a witch trial in the 1600s shows the scales at Oudewater in the Netherlands. The suspect, wearing the lightest of gowns, was first searched for any hidden weights, to make sure she was not trying to be heavier than she was. Then she was weighed.

▶ PUBLIC HUMILIATION

In the USA in 1692, an outbreak of witch-hunting erupted in Salem, Massachusetts. This painting by the American artist T. H. Matteson shows a suspect in the Salem witch trials undergoing the humiliating search for the Devil's Mark. Blemishes such as moles or scars were supposed to have been left on a witch by the Devil's claws or teeth. Two people faint in horror when a couple of meddlesome matrons point to the supposed blemishes of the accused girl.

▶ THE WITCHFINDER GENERAL

Matthew Hopkins questions two witches surrounded by their familiars. Hopkins was England's most famous witch-hunter, and even called himself the Witchfinder General. He scoured the counties of eastern England from 1645 to 1646, looking for victims. He was paid for each arrest, and made a profitable living, before he was discredited as a fraud and forced to retire. Torture was forbidden by English law, so Hopkins chose swimming, pricking tests, and depriving people of sleep to force confessions from his victims. During Hopkins's search, more women were hanged for witchcraft in a year than they had been over the whole previous 100 years.

▶ PRICKING STICKS

One telltale sign for witchcraft was supposed to be an area on the body where the witch felt no pain. A suspect was stripped and poked all over with a sharp implement, called a pricking stick. This collection of pricking sticks includes one which has a blade, like a theatrical dagger, which would retract harmlessly into the handle if pressed against someone. Some witch hunters used pricking sticks like this, so that they could be sure of condemning their victims. A witch-finder could stick this in a suspect and draw no blood, then claim that she felt no pain. These were seen as clear signs that she possessed demonic powers.

◀ UNDER ARREST

A frail old woman is arrested for witchcraft, surrounded by six armed men. Her haggard, stooped appearance and ragged clothes agree with what many people at the time expected a witch to look like. This illustration comes from an account of the Salem witch trials in Massachusetts. The witch-hunting outbreak was caused when a group of young girls accused other villagers of witchcraft. It may have begun as a prank, but 141 people were arrested, and 20 were executed.

◀ TRIAL BY WATER

Another test for witchcraft was to be thrown into a river. If the suspect sank, then she was innocent. If she floated, she was being rejected by the water as an evil witch. In this English woodcut of 1613, the suspect Mary Sutton is going through this ordeal. But she is fastened to a rope held by two men, who will save her from drowning should the river prove her innocence.

Trial and Punishment

O nce sufficient evidence had been gathered to convince the authorities that a suspect was a witch, a grisly process of trial and punishment was set in motion. A successful prosecution (accusation of criminal action) depended on the suspect admitting that he or she was guilty. Most of them were probably completely bewildered by the charges, but they were all too aware that death was the punishment if they were found guilty. Therefore, suspects were not likely to confess unless they were forced to do so. This was sometimes done by torturing them until they admitted whatever it was that their accusers wanted them to say.

Before around 1450, there were no witch trials. This was because people were not often accused of witchcraft, and also because the law made prosecution difficult. A private individual was allowed to bring a case to court, but if the accused was found not guilty, then the accuser would be severely punished. As the Church became more concerned with stamping out heresy, the law was changed, and the Church or the Government acted as both prosecutor and judge. A confession extracted through torture was enough evidence to send victims to their deaths.

▲ INSTRUMENTS OF TORTURE

A frightening collection of torture equipment and tools of execution was used at the Bamberg witch trials in Germany in the 1600s. Among the items are a stake, gallows, executioner's sword, stocks, thumbscrews, and a pillory. Such devices were blessed by a priest before they were put to use, to show that the punishment about to be given had been approved by the Church.

▲ COTTON MATHER

The Reverend Cotton Mather, a Massachusetts minister, was one of the leading supporters of the Salem witch trials. After the trials he published a pamphlet justifying the hysteria, called *The Wonders of the Invisible World*. Mather was a highly educated and respected man. The fact that an educated man could believe in the witches of Salem shows the attitudes and prejudices of the times.

◀ THE SALEM WITCHES

As two anxious suspects face the court, witnesses point hysterically at them, declaring they can see a flock of yellow birds around their heads. This engraving of 1892 captures some of the atmosphere of the Salem witch trials of 1692 in Massachusetts. Several young girls of the town claimed that they had been bewitched by a West Indian slave. This was the only occasion in which the USA experienced the same kind of witch-hunting frenzy that had gripped Europe.

ROUGH JUSTICE

Four unfortunate prisoners, wearing robes and hats designed to humiliate them, sit before the court, accused of witchcraft and heresy. All four were most likely tortured to obtain the confessions used as evidence against them. This painting is by the Spanish artist, Goya, and is called *A Scene from the Inquisition*. The Inquisition was set up in 1233 to enforce the authority of the Catholic Church and to prevent the spread of alternative beliefs. Any threat, real or imagined, was dealt with ruthlessly. The Inquisition claimed hundreds of thousands of victims.

MAKING HIM TALK

A woodcut of the 1400s shows a suspect being prepared for a method of torture called strappado. With his hands tied behind his back, he will be suspended from a chain with a weight tied to his feet. Three clerks sit at a table ready to record his confession, while another official addresses him.

LAST CONVICTION

Jane Wenham of Hertford was the last person to be convicted of witchcraft in England. At her trial in 1712, she was sentenced to death. The judge at the trial had no intention of sending her to the gallows, and requested a pardon from Queen Anne. The pardon was granted, but Jane Wenham had to be hidden from an angry mob that had gathered to kill her themselves.

BURNED AT THE STAKE

Most witches were executed by being burned at the stake. The punishment was intended to be a taste of the flames of hell that were to come. In this German engraving from 1555, an evil spirit has already come to claim one of the three witches being burned to death. To the right of the picture lies a dead child. Perhaps the women were accused of causing his death by evil magic. In the distance, an executioner prepares to behead another witch. Beheading was at least a quicker, less agonizing way to die. Witches were also hanged from the gallows, another slow death that could be slow and horribly painful.

A Magic Seal

Throughout history, seals have been used to fasten things that should not be opened, such as the door of a tomb, or a secret message. Seals were believed to have magic powers from the special inscriptions and symbols that were molded or etched into them, and for this reason they were used to ward off evil magic. In this project, a wax-like seal is used to close a letter written on a scroll. The symbols on the seal come from the art of alchemy, in which men would try to discover a magical formula to turn ordinary metals into gold. The box opposite shows what they represent.

1 Take a lump of self-hardening clay and place it on a work board. Use a rolling pin to roll out a ¼-inch thick piece of clay, about 4 x 4 inches.

2 Measure the circumference and half the length of an empty candy tube. Then cut a slab from the clay of the same measurements.

You will need: self-hardening clay, work board, rolling pin, ruler, small empty candy tube (or similar) cut in half, modeling tool (or blunt knife), small dish, glue, glue brush, craft knife, red oven-bake modeling material, thick dark ribbon.

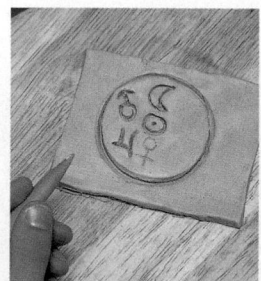

4 Use the modeling tool to draw alchemical symbols in the clay inside the circle. Make light marks, so that you can change the design if you want to.

5 When you are happy with your design, go over it again with the modeling tool, making heavier marks. Keep your design as neat as possible.

6 Turn the slab over very carefully. Then spread glue all over the card tube. Roll the clay slab around the tube, being careful not to smudge the design.

These two ancient star-shaped symbols were often used to ward off evil. The six-pointed star on the left is called a hexagram, and is sometimes known as the Seal of Solomon or the Star of David. The star on the right is called a pentagram, meaning that it has five points.

9 Roll the dry clay tube over the red disk shape, so that the alchemy symbols leave a good imprint. If the print is uneven, smooth and repeat.

10 Use the modeling tool to trim any excess clay outside the imprinted circle. Bake it in an oven, following the instructions on the package.

3 Take a small, circular dish that fits neatly inside the area of the slab you have cut. Press the dish gently into the clay to leave a circular impression.

ALCHEMY SYMBOLS

 Sun = gold

 Mercury = mercury

 Mars = iron

ħ Saturn = lead

 Moon = silver

 Venus = copper

4 Jupiter = tin

Alchemists used these astrological symbols in their secret writings to represent different metals.

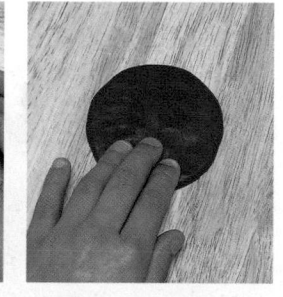

In the past, seals for letters were made of red wax. Molten wax was poured on to the letter, and the seal pressed into the wax to leave an impression.

7 Use a craft knife to trim any excess clay. Use your fingers to smooth the joint where the ends of the clay meet. Leave to one side to dry thoroughly.

8 Take some red oven-bake modeling material and put it on the board. Use your hands to squash and roll it into a circular disk shape.

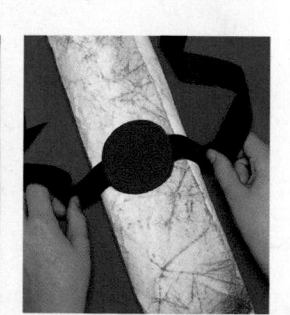

11 Leave the seal to cool. Spread a narrow strip of glue on the back of the seal, and stick it in the middle of a piece of thick ribbon. Leave this to dry.

12 Use the seal to secure an important piece of paper you want to keep, such as a letter. Roll the paper into a scroll, and tie the seal around the middle.

Shamans and Magic

Many people all over the world live in tribal communities. A tribe is a group of people who often share common ancestors and a common territory and culture. Most tribal peoples have healers called shamans, who play an important role in their society. Shamans are also called witch doctors or medicine men. Many shamans are men, but sometimes women fulfill this role.

Shamans have been highly valued members of tribal societies for more than 30,000 years, and this early existence may be the first ever indication of organized religion. Some shamans have a guardian spirit that is the source of their power. They go into a trance-like state, in which they can communicate with spirits and draw on their enormous power.

Shamans from different tribes share a great many similarities with each other in their abilities and their ways of working. The shaman uses his or her power to heal members of the tribe who are sick. Rituals that involve music and dancing, and eating and drinking, are used to see into the future and to bring prosperity to the tribe—for example, by insuring that hunting expeditions are successful.

▶ OLD BEAR

Old Bear was a shaman of the Mandan people of the Great Plains of North America. This painting of him from 1832 is the work of the American artist, George Catlin. In Old Bear's hands are two wand-like batons, decorated with feathers and furs. He also carries healing herbs tucked into the animal hide tied around his middle. The Mandan tribe and their culture were almost wiped out by a smallpox epidemic five years after this painting was completed.

◀ ZULU WITCH DOCTOR

A female Zulu witch doctor from South Africa is working as an oracle, predicting the future with the aid of her spirit helpers. Belief in the magic of shamans and witch doctors is extremely strong in some parts of the world. In their healing roles, witch doctors use their power to diagnose and cure diseases.

▶ FALSE FACE MASK

Shamans from the Iroquois tribe, of the East Coast of North America, wore elaborately painted wood and horsehair masks in ceremonial dances. The wearers took on the power of the spirits that the masks represented, during healing rituals. They believed the mask offered them a way to enter the spirit world and to identify with the spirits.

▲ PAINTING IN THE SAND

Navajo shamans of the southwestern USA used colored sands to create pictures on the floor of a patient's home. The paintings showed powerful spirits from Navajo myths, and played a vital role in healing rituals. During the ceremonies, the patient would sit within the painting, while the shaman summoned spirit powers with sacred chants and asked them to cure the patient. After the ritual, the painting was destroyed.

▲ SUMMONING DRUM

Music and rhythm are an important part of shamanic rituals. Drums and rattles are used by many tribes. This leather and wooden drum was used by the Magar tribe of Nepal. The sound of the music is believed to summon the spirit guardians and guides of the shaman, and also helps the shaman enter a trance so that he or she can communicate with the spirits.

◀ MEDICINE MAN

Carrying the tools of his trade and his bedding on his back, this Chinese medicine man wanders the footpaths of the Himalayas, looking for business. He may have various animal parts for sale, including bones, shells, skulls, horns, and claws. They may be used for healing, or as lucky charms to ward off evil spirits.

▲ ABORIGINAL HEALER

An Aboriginal (native) Australian medicine man of the 1900s has decorated his body with magical markings. The Aborigines believe that serious illness is sometimes caused by bad magic. Someone becomes ill because an invisible spear or stone is thrust into them, leaving a splinter or bone that will kill them. The medicine man is called on to extract this splinter or bone. Aboriginal medicine men are also supposed to be able to see and speak to the spirit doubles of people. If someone is murdered, a medicine man visits the scene of the crime, speaks to the dead body's spirit, and names the culprit.

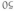

A Shaman's Mask

From North America to Africa and Asia, many tribal rituals involve the wearing of elaborate masks, often as part of a ceremonial dance. These are intended to enable the wearer to identify and communicate with particular spirits.

The mask in this project is based on an original one used by shamans in Sri Lanka. The original mask was made out of wood and is supposed to represent a serpent demon called Garayaka. This dangerous demon is said to cause illnesses and is driven from the body of the patient in a purification ritual conducted by the shaman.

You will need: ruler, white card, black felt-tipped pen, scissors, pencil, masking tape, pair of compasses, newspaper, small mixing bowl, spoon, flour, water, fine sandpaper, thick paintbrushes, white emulsion paint, black, red, orange, yellow, and white acrylic paints, fine paintbrushes, thin elastic.

1 Shown above are templates for the main part of the mask and the cobras. You will need three cobras.

5 Using a pencil and ruler, copy the cobra head template three times onto the white card. Follow the measurements shown on the template. Cut out the shapes.

6 Use masking tape or Scotch tape to attach the cobra heads to the top of the mask. Gently bend the heads forward, like a real cobra's head.

7 Use a pair of compasses to draw two circles 5 inches across onto card. Draw a circle ¾ inch across in the middle. Cut out both large circles, then cut out the middles.

12 When the papier-mâché is dry, sand it down with fine sandpaper. Then use a thick paintbrush to apply white emulsion paint all over the mask.

13 When the paint is completely dry, use a pencil to draw the features on the face. Draw patterns on the ears and cobra heads, too.

14 Paint the mask as shown. Use a thick paintbrush to paint big areas of color. Use a fine paintbrush for finer details, such as the teeth and the scales.

15 When the paint is dry, make a hole on both sides of the mask. Pull a piece of elastic through from the back of each hole, and knot at the front.

Shamans wear costumes and masks in rituals to help them to assume the characters of the spirits more fully. The three snake's heads on this particular mask represent the serpent demon that the shaman is trying to drive away.

8 Use tape to fix the card circles to either side of the mask, to make a pair of ears. Make sure the pieces touch, but do not overlap, the face.

9 Scrunch up newspaper into long sausage shapes for the mouth and eyebrows. Scrunch up two newspaper balls for the eyeballs. Tape into place.

10 To make the nose, draw a flat triangular shape onto card and cut it out. Make a fold down the middle, then tape it in position on the mask.

11 Mix a paste of flour and water in a bowl into a thick batter. Dip newspaper strips in the paste. Cover the mask in about three layers of papier-mâché.

A beautifully carved and painted mask from Mongolia represents the Spirit of the Barren Mountain. It is used in a sacred dance that was probably first performed by shamans.

4 Hold the mask up to your face, and make marks with a pencil where your eyes and nose are. Now draw the nose and eye shapes in place and cut them out.

3 Use a pair of scissors to carefully cut around the shape of the shaman's mask. Try to keep the shape as smooth as possible.

2 Using a ruler and a black felt-tipped pen, measure and draw a basic mask shape on the piece of white card. Use the template from step 1.

Fairy-tale Magic

It is through fairy tales, myths, and legends that our images of witches and wizards are formed. From the earliest times, right up until the latest films and computer games, witches and wizards continue to capture people's imagination. Most of these stories show witches as people to be feared and avoided. In earlier times, fables about them would have added to the hostility felt toward witchcraft. In recent times, witches have become more friendly figures. The child-eating, cackling monsters of fairy tales have been replaced by good natured softies such as Jan Pienkowski's Meg and her cat Mog.

Wizards, however, have never attracted the same hostility as witches. From figures such as Merlin at the court of King Arthur, to Gandalf in Tolkien's *The Lord of the Rings*, wizards have almost always been heroes. The Harry Potter books by J. K. Rowling, with their comical and exciting stories of children training to be wizards and witches, are a far cry from the cruel images of earlier times.

▲ DR. FAUSTUS

Dr. Faustus, inside a magic circle with a spell book in his hand, summons a demon. In the story, Faustus sells his soul to the Devil in exchange for 24 years of unlimited wisdom and pleasure. As the year of his damnation draws nearer, however, Faustus grows increasingly fearful. On the night that the Devil comes to claim his soul, a fierce wind swirls around his house. His neigbors hear terrified screams. In the morning, they find his crumpled body in a dung heap, and his brains, teeth, eyeballs, and blood are splattered over the walls.

◀ MACBETH

Surrounded by malevolent crows, three hags prepare to meet the hero of William Shakespeare's play, *Macbeth*. In the play, the Scottish lord, Macbeth, is confronted by the witches on his travels, and they predict that he is destined to be King of Scotland. Great tragedy and bloodshed follow, and Macbeth is eventually killed. Shakespeare included the witches to appeal to King James I, who was interested in witchcraft. To mention the play's name in a theater is said to bring bad luck.

▲ A SLEEPING SPELL

In the story *Sleeping Beauty*, a beautiful princess is cursed by a witch. She pricks her finger on the witch's spindle, sending her into a charmed sleep. She is unable to wake up until a handsome prince comes to the rescue and wakes her with a kiss. Many old folk tales such as this were retold by two German brothers called Jacob and Wilhelm Grimm. Their stories, published in the 1800s, were tremendously popular all over the world, and are still told to children today.

◀ HANSEL AND GRETEL

A crucial scene from *Hansel and Gretel*, a German fairy tale retold by the Grimm brothers, shows Gretel pushing a wicked witch into an oven. In the story, Hansel and Gretel become lost in the woods. They come across an odd gingerbread house and are tempted inside by a peculiar, but kindly, old lady. Alas, their host is a witch who intends to eat them for her supper. Due to Gretel's quick actions, the children manage to escape.

▶ INTO THE INK

This illustration shows a famous magician called Agrippa punishing three naughty boys by plunging them into an inkwell. It appears in a book of cautionary tales by the German writer Heinrich Hoffman, published in 1876. In the book, children who misbehave come to a gruesome end. Agrippa was a real person. He was a scholar in the 1500s who wrote books on magic. He was believed to be a sorcerer and to practice black magic.

▶ BABA YAGA

The Russian witch Baba Yaga, shown here riding her broomstick, loved to roast and eat people, especially children. Baba Yaga lived in a house in the woods, which was ringed with stakes topped by human skulls. The house was built on chicken and dogs' legs, and could turn around at her command. This illustration comes from a British children's book published in 1913, called *Old Peter's Russian Tales*.

◀ BLACK CATS AND BROOMSTICKS

Some of the most charming and atmospheric children's book illustrations were drawn by an artist called Arthur Rackham in the early 1900s. His illustrations for *Ingoldsby Legends* show the classic image of witches with pointed hats, broomsticks, and black cats. *Ingoldsby Legends* was a collection of country tales and medieval legends written in the mid-1800s, by a clergyman called Richard Harris Barham.

Screen Witches

The movies are a wonderful way of telling a scary story. In a darkened room and with a hushed, expectant audience, a visit to the movies is a spellbinding experience. Unsurprisingly, witches have always been popular subjects and have fascinated filmmakers and audiences throughout the history of movies. Movies, such as the 1922 Swedish movie, *Witchcraft Through the Ages* and *The Blair Witch Project* of 1999, which made a big impact when they were released, were designed to thrill and horrify audiences.

Like the images from myths and legends, witches in movies and television are shown either as sinister, ugly, old crones, such as the one in *Snow White and the Seven Dwarfs*, or as beautiful and determined, like Samantha from the popular TV series, *Bewitched*. Whatever they look like, all of these witches have the ability to practice magic for good or evil. The image of witches is gradually becoming more positive. The modern-day equivalents of the hags that our ancestors believed practiced evil magic in our midst are more likely to be kindly, rather than frightening characters.

A POISONED APPLE
Snow White looks suspicious when a warty old woman tries to tempt her with a poisonous apple. Walt Disney's 1937 film is a cartoon adaptation of a Grimms' fairy tale. Disney described the witch as a mixture of William Shakespeare's Lady Macbeth and the big bad wolf from *Little Red Riding Hood*. More than 60 years later, she still has the power to frighten people. The witch is really Snow White's stepmother, the wicked queen, who has disguised herself with a spell.

I MARRIED A WITCH ▶
In spite of the pointed hat, black cape, and broomstick, the film star, Veronica Lake, fails to look sinister and ugly in the 1942 film, *I Married a Witch*. She plays a witch who seeks revenge on a politician whose ancestors had her burned at the stake in a previous life.

▼ BLOCKBUSTER
The 1939 version of *The Wizard of Oz* was the most successful of of three films based on L. Frank Baum's children's novel. The heroine, Dorothy (played in the 1939 version by Judy Garland), is swept away in a tornado and lands in the fantasy land of Oz, where she is tormented by the Wicked Witch of the North. She makes friends and has many adventures with the Scarecrow, the Tin Man, and the Cowardly Lion.

▶ GANDALF THE WIZARD

In 1978, J. R. R. Tolkien's classic trilogy of books, *The Lord of the Rings*, was made into a film. The part of Gandalf the wizard (shown here in a poster for the film) was played by American actor William Squire. The film, which is a mixture of animation and live action, covers only the first two parts of the trilogy. It is the story of a band of travelers who seek to defeat an evil sorcerer and his armies with the aid of a powerful, but evil, magic ring.

◀ BEWITCHED

Elizabeth Montgomery played the witch Samantha in the US TV series *Bewitched*, which was first screened from 1964 to 1972. One of TV's classic comedies, the series has been shown in many different countries around the world. Samantha was married to a down-to-earth husband, Darrin, who disapproved of his wife using her magic powers. Samantha famously twitched her nose to work her spells. More often than not, she used her powers to correct the mess left behind by her meddling family. Still popular today, *Bewitched* was originally inspired by the film *I Married a Witch*.

◀ MERLIN THE MAGICIAN

In the 1981 film *Excalibur*, a version of the legend of King Arthur, Nicol Williamson played court magician Merlin. He battles with Arthur's half-sister and enemy, Morgan le Fay. Williamson, seen here wearing a steel skull cap, instead of the more traditional pointed wizard hat, portrays Merlin as a bustling, eccentric figure. The film was based on Sir Thomas Malory's book, *Morte d'Arthur*.

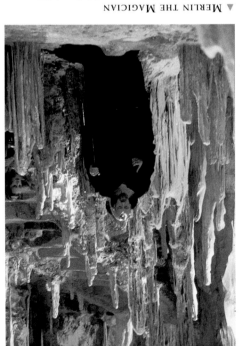

◀ THE WITCHES

The actress Anjelica Huston is unrecognizable underneath her grotesque makeup. She played a wicked witch in the 1990 film of Roald Dahl's book, *The Witches*. In the movie, the witch plans to poison all the children in Britain with a powerful magic potion. Only a little boy (who has been turned into a mouse) and his grandma can stop her evil intentions. Like many of Dahl's stories, the film is dark and menacing, but is also very humorous.

A Halloween Feast

Halloween, on October 31st, is the night most closely connected with witchcraft. In pre-Christian times, this was when the beginning of winter was celebrated. Halloween's association with witches stems from the legend that the sun is so low in the sky on that day, the gates of the underworld have to be opened to let in the light. When the gates open, demons and spectres spill out to plague the Earth.

The ritual of "trick or treat" takes place on Halloween. Children dressed as witches and ghouls visit houses, demanding candy or money. In return, they promise not to play a trick on the person they visit. In this project, you can find out how to make some scary food for a Halloween party.

For the cat and bat cookies you will need: card, pencil, scissors, mixing bowl, butter, sugar, wooden spoon, 1 egg, flour, black food coloring, chopping board, rolling pin, blunt knife, baking tray, wire rack, red and green frosting.

For the potato face you will need: 1 large potato, spoon, mixing bowl, green food coloring, butter, grated cheese, salt, pepper, chopping board, 1 carrot, 1 red pepper, spring onions, 1 cooked sausage, sliced mushrooms, mustard cress, a handful of grated American cheese.

For the drink you will need: paintbrush, glue, colored plastic straws, toy spiders, tall drinking glass, small plate, ice cream, soda, chocolate sprinkles.

1 Scale these two templates onto a thick piece of card and cut out. You could also make other shapes, such as jack-o'-lanterns and ghosts.

2 Put ½ cup butter or margarine in a mixing bowl. Add ½ cup sugar. Stir with a wooden spoon until the dough is fluffy and creamy.

These cookies would make a perfect treat for trick or treating on Halloween. This custom recalls days long gone when people were wary of offending local witches, in case the witch placed a curse upon them.

3 Cut the carrot into strips. Cut the red pepper in a zigzag for teeth. Cut the ends of the onions into fan shapes. Slice the sausage. Fry the mushrooms in butter.

4 Use the vegetables and sausage to make a face and hair on the potato. Sprinkle grated cheese around the potato face to make it even more tasty.

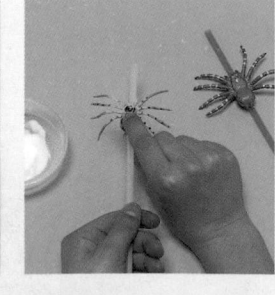

1 For the drink: Use the paintbrush to put a dab of glue near the top of each plastic straw. Fix a toy spider firmly in place on each straw.

2 Put the glass on a small plate. Put 3 or 4 tablespoons of ice-cream in the glass. (Chocolate-mint chip looks good, because it is a ghoulish green color.)

3 Add 1 egg beaten, 1¼ cups flour, and a few drops of black food coloring. Mix until it forms a dough. Stir really well, so that the food coloring blends in.

4 Roll the dough out on a board to about ½-in thick. Put the bat and cat templates on the dough, and carefully cut around them with a blunt knife.

5 Roll out the leftover dough again and cut out more shapes. Place the animal shapes on a nonstick baking tray. Bake for 20 minutes at 250°F.

6 When the shapes are baked, remove from the oven and cool on a rack. Mix the red and green frosting. Use your fingers to add the bats' and cats' features.

1 Ask an adult to bake a large potato. When it has cooled, use a knife to cut off the top. Use a spoon to scoop the insides into a bowl. Add green coloring.

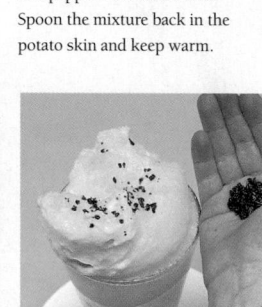

2 Add ¼ cup butter, ¼ cup grated cheese, and season with salt and pepper. Mix with a fork. Spoon the mixture back in the potato skin and keep warm.

3 Pour a soda drink over the ice cream. Limeade works well because it is ghastly green, like the ice cream. Add enough so that it really foams up.

4 Sprinkle little flakes of chocolate over the top. You could add mini-marshmallows or nonpareils instead. Stick the straws into the drink.

With these delicious treats, your party is bound to be a success. Make enough cookies, potato faces, and ghoulish drinks for everyone you have invited. Don't forget to decorate the room with some really scary trimmings.

Modern Witchcraft

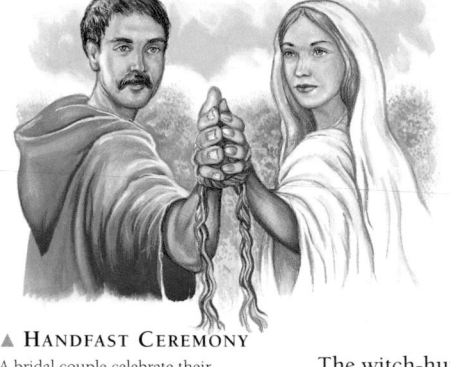

A bridal couple celebrate their marriage in a modern witchcraft ceremony. They are taking part in a ritual called handfasting. The couple have made a colorful, three-strand fiber band that binds them together. The three strands stand for the bride, the groom, and their relationship. If, later in life, the couple decide to separate, the union can be undone with another witchcraft ceremony called handparting.

All crazes eventually die down, and witch-hunting was no exception. As the 1700s dawned, the persecutions that had claimed so many lives over the previous 300 years, gradually began to grind to a halt. In England, the last witch was convicted in 1712, but was given a royal pardon. In Scotland, a witch was burned in 1727. There were some executions in France in 1745, and finally, in Bavaria in 1775, the last witch to be executed in Europe was beheaded.

The witch-hunts had brought terrible turmoil, and whole communities had been devastated, but times were changing. Science was in fashion, and an era that became known as the Age of Reason arrived. As the 1700s passed, the feudal societies of Europe began to modernize themselves. There was a general drift in population from countryside to town. In the 1800s, a world of roads and railways, cities and factories began to take shape. However, interest in magic is still present in modern Western society, and many people practice different versions of magic and witchcraft. Today, witchcraft involves honoring the earth and nature and is a far cry from the witchcraft imagined by the Christian Church during the witch-hunts.

◀ **LOCKED IN THE STOCKS**
In the 1700s and 1800s, people were still prosecuted for witchcraft, but they were more likely to be guilty of trickery and preying on vulnerable people. Their fate was not the stake or gallows. Instead, they were locked up in a public place in a pillory or stocks (in which their feet were locked). Then they were a target for any passer-by who felt like pelting them with rotten fruit and vegetables.

TALKING TO THE DEAD ▶
In the late 1800s, spiritualism became fashionable. This is a belief that people can communicate with the spirits of the dead at a gathering called a seance. At this seance in New York in 1887, a guitar somehow floats in the air, although everyone present is holding hands. Spiritualism continued to be hugely popular in the early 1900s, particularly after World War I. Widows, mothers, and children were desperate to contact the millions of soldiers who had died in the war.

▶ **INITIATION CEREMONY**

Modern-day witches are forming a magic circle as part of an initiation ceremony. Because the term witchcraft has such bad associations for many people, they prefer to use the term Wicca (an old English word meaning witch) to describe their activities. Today, Wiccan groups can be found all over the world, especially in Europe, North America, Australia, and Japan.

▶ **TOOLS OF WITCHCRAFT**

Those who practice witchcraft today use tools and objects in their spells and rituals. Here, you can see two of them. The chalice is a feminine symbol. It holds wine or water. The knife, or athane, is a masculine symbol, which is used to direct psychic energy.

▶ **THE FATHER OF MODERN WITCHCRAFT**

Gerald Gardner is sometimes called the Father of Modern Witchcraft. For many years, Gardner was a British government worker employed as a plantation manager in Southeast Asia. In 1939, he returned to England and claimed to have been initiated into a secret group called the Wicca. In fact, he probably created modern witchcraft. The witchcraft laws were abolished in 1951, and in 1954, Gardner published a book about Wicca (modern witchcraft) called *Witchcraft Today*. This and his other books were tremendously influential. They formed the idea of the witch as someone who practiced a pre-Christian religion.

▶ **MODERN MAGICIAN**

The English magician, Aleister Crowley, poses dramatically for the camera, dressed in ceremonial robes and surrounded by the ritual implements of his magic. Crowley had a peculiar career. Hounded by Britain's popular newspapers, which described him as the wickedest man alive, he died a drug addict in 1947. He remains a fascinating and even honored figure, however, to those who practice magic today. He wrote more than 100 books on the subject and his motto, "Do what thou wilt, shall be the whole of the law," has been adopted as a way of life by many modern magicians.

Timeline

Magic has been part of human culture since society began, and it still plays an important role in some societies today. Over the centuries, attitudes toward witches have changed. One of the most disturbing periods in history was between 1450 and 1700, when witches were feared and violently persecuted.

Before 3000 B.C.

30,000 B.C. POSSIBLY the first evidence of tribal shamans found in cave paintings and archaeological remains.

3000–1000 B.C. ANCIENT Egyptian civilization flourished. Magic spells and rituals are part of everyday life.

prehistoric cave painting, possibly of a shaman, from France

3000 B.C. PALM READING first practiced in China.

2000 B.C.–A.D. 100

2000–146 B.C. Ancient GREEK civilization flourishes. Many legends from Greece concerning witchcraft, such as shape-changing, familiars, and horned gods, will become part of Western European folklore.

500 B.C. ALCHEMY begins in Ancient China.

c. A.D. 100 THE TRADITIONAL text of the Old Testament is translated into Greek by Jewish authorities. In it are the words, "Thou shall not suffer a witch to live." This phrase is used by later Christians to justify their persecution of witches.

A.D. 100–800 MISSIONARIES convert Europe from pagan religions to Christianity.

1400–1431

c. 1400s A FRENCH illustration shows the first known images of witches flying on broomsticks.

1404–1440 LIFE OF GILLES de Rais, one of the most notorious sorcerers and alchemists who lived in the Middle Ages.

French illustration of a witch flying on a broomstick

1428 HERETIC TRIALS in the Dauphine region of France. 167 people are burned at the stake over the next 20 years.

1431 JOAN OF ARC burned as a heretic.

1450-1484

c. 1450 THE BEGINNING OF mass persecution of witches in Europe.

1459 WITCH TRIALS in Arras, France. Hundreds are implicated as mass hysteria grips the town.

1473–1541 LIFE OF PARACELSUS, the famous Swiss alchemist and medical scientist.

1484 POPE INNOCENT VIII issues a papal bull used to authorize witch-hunting in Germany.

Christian cross

1485–1503

c. 1485 SIR THOMAS MALORY writes *Morte d'Arthur*—tales of the legendary King Arthur.

1486 MALLEUS MALEFICARUM (Hammer of Witches) is published. It was a witch judge's manual and was hostile to women.

c. 1500 RELIGIOUS RIVALRY and warfare in Europe inspire greater persecution of witches.

alchemical symbols

1503–1566 LIFE of Nostradamus, French healer and astrologer.

1591–1604

1591 NICOLAS REMY is chief prosecutor of witches in Lorraine, France. He sends over 900 to be executed.

1597 JAMES VI OF SCOTLAND'S *Demonology* published It hardens prejudice against witchcraft in England.

1603–1606 300 PEOPLE sent to be burned as witches in Fulda, southern Germany, by the infamous judge, Balthasar Ross.

1603–1625 REIGN OF JAMES I of England and James VI of Scotland.

1604 CHRISTOPHER MARLOWE'S famous play *Dr. Faustus* is performed.

1606–1620

1606 SHAKESPEARE'S PLAY *Macbeth* features the three most famous witches in literature.

1609 PIERRE DE LANCRE, chief prosecutor in Southwest France, claims 30,000 people in his district are witches. He also says 100,000 people attend sabbats in Bordeaux. He sends 600 suspects to their deaths.

1618–1648 THE THIRTY YEARS War rages in central Europe. Witch-hunting is at its height.

witch's hex doll, used for spell making

1620s 900 PEOPLE BURNED as witches in Würzburg, Germany.

1625–1727

c. 1625 600 MEN AND WOMEN burned as witches at Bamburg, Germany.

1626 COMPENDIUM MALEFICARUM (Handbook of Witches) is published. It does much to fan the flames of witch-hunting hysteria.

1631 FRIEDRICH VON SPEE publishes *Cautio Criminalis* (Precautions for Prosecutors) in Germany, opposing witch-hunting hysteria.

1642–1727 LIFE OF SIR ISAAC Newton —Britain's most distinguished scientist and alchemist.

Newton's famous book on the laws of motion

1812–1821

1812–1822 THE BROTHERS GRIMM fairy tales are published in three volumes. They contain several stories concerning witches, which introduce future generations of children to the images of a witch as a crooked-nosed, warty-faced evil old hag.

a witch's cat from a fairy tale

1817–1821 A POLTERGEIST supposedly persecutes the Bell family in Tennessee. One of the family is killed. People believed in evil magic at the time, so the ghost became known as the Bell Witch.

1850–1922

c. 1850 SPIRITUALISM becomes popular, in which people try to contact the souls of their dead friends and relatives.

1875–1947 LIFE OF MAGICIAN Aleister Crowley. He achieves a reputation in the newspapers as the wickedest man alive.

1883–1964 LIFE OF GERALD GARDNER. Considered to be the father of modern witchcraft.

ritual objects of modern witchcraft

1922 THE SWEDISH FILM *Witchcraft through the Ages* is made. A silent horror film, it is banned for many years.

1937–1950

1937 DISNEY releases *Snow White*, an animated film of the well-known Grimm's fairy tale.

1939 THE FILM of *The Wizard of Oz* is released, based on the writer L. Frank Baum's popular novel of fantasy adventure.

1937–1955 J.R.R. TOLKIEN publishes his fantasy novels, *The Hobbit* and the *Lord of the Rings* trilogy, featuring the kindly wizard Gandalf.

astrological symbols

A.D. 367–550

A.D. 367. FIRST ORGANIZED WITCH HUNT by Emperor Valerian in Rome.

A.D. 391 CHRISTIANITY BECOMES the official religion of the Roman Empire.

c. A.D. 450 LIFE OF THE LEGENDARY Arthur, King of Britain, who was aided by his court magician Merlin.

A.D. 476 FALL OF ROME. Pagan and Christian practices continue to coexist in Europe.

c. A.D. 550 LEGEND OF Greek monk Theophilus, who sells his soul to the Devil. This story will later be known as Dr. Faustus.

A.D. 550–1174

c. A.D. 750 ALCHEMICAL IDEAS reach the Middle East from China and India.

A.D. 787 EMPEROR CHARLEMAGNE issues a decree calling for the execution of anyone discovered making sacrifices to the Devil.

c. 1050 CONTACT WITH ARAB countries brings alchemical ideas to Europe.

1174 HENRY II of ENGLAND's wife Eleanor suspected of practicing witchcraft.

1193–1324

1193–1280 LIFE OF Bishop Albertus Magnus, a scientist and student of magic.

1233 THE CATHOLIC CHURCH founds the Inquisition to persecute heretics.

1320 A FAILED ASSASSINATION attempt on Pope John XXII is said to involve poisoning and witchcraft. Persecution of heretics by the Church intensifies.

1323 A MAGICIAN IS BURNED alive in Paris.

1324 PETRONILLA DE MEATH is the first person condemned to be burned in Ireland.

a witch burned at the stake

1520–1536

1520s SPANISH EXPLORER Cabez de Vaca witnesses Native North American shamans curing the sick.

1527 BIRTH OF JOHN DEE, Alchemist, Sorcerer, and Astrologer to the court of Queen Elizabeth I of England.

1532 THE CAROLINA CODE is issued in Germany. It imposes torture and death for witchcraft.

1536 ANNE BOLEYN, wife of King Henry VIII of England, is executed. Henry ruined her reputation by accusing her of witchcraft, among other things.

a necklace used by a Native North American shaman

1555–1565

1555 NOSTRADAMUS publishes Centuries—his famous predictions.

1562 THE CATHOLIC CHURCH announces its intention to win back Germany from Protestantism at the Council of Trent. Persecution of witches intensifies.

1563 ELIZABETH I of England passes statute against witchcraft.

1565 THE FIRST WITCHCRAFT trial in England takes place against three women from Chelmsford. Two of them are hanged.

1576–1590

1576–1612 REIGN OF RUDOLF II, Holy Roman Emperor and patron of alchemists in Prague.

1585 REGINALD SCOT's book, The Discoverie of Witchcraft, attempts to discredit witch-hunting. It has very little affect on attitudes.

1589 133 WITCHES BURNED in a single day in Quedlinburg in Saxony.

1590 NORTH BERWICK witches of Scotland accused of trying to kill King James VI.

witches in company of the Devil

1645–1684

1645–6 WITCHFINDER GENERAL Matthew Hopkins conducts his witch-hunts in eastern England. He is discredited and dies within a year.

1647 MATTHEW HOPKINS publishes a booklet called Discovery of Witchcraft shortly before his death, to try to justify his witch-hunts.

1669 85 WITCHES BURNED at Mora, Sweden.

1669 THE ALCHEMIST HENNIG BRAND accidentally discovers the chemical phosphorus.

1684 ALICE MOLLAND is the last woman to be executed as a witch in England.

1692–1727

1692 SALEM WITCH TRIALS, the most infamous outbreak of witch-hunting in North America. The trials result in 19 executions.

1700s GREATER SCIENTIFIC KNOWLEDGE and changing social conditions lead to a decline in the belief in witchcraft, and persecution gradually stops.

1712 JANE WENHAM is the last witch to be convicted in English court. She is given a royal pardon.

1727 JANET HORNE is the last witch to be executed in Scotland.

1736–1787

1736 NEW LAWS IN ENGLAND remove penalties for witchcraft and replace them with punishments for fraudulent fortune-telling, and other hoaxes relating to the practice of magic.

1745 FATHER LOUIS DEBARAZ is the last witch to be executed in France.

1775 ANNA MARIA SCHWAGEL of Bavaria is the last to be executed in Europe.

1787 ALL WITCHCRAFT laws in Austria are repealed.

a witch is punished in a pillory

1951–1976

1951 WITCHCRAFT LAWS repealed in Britain, and witchcraft is now legal. The revival of witchcraft as a kind of pagan religion in Britain, the USA, and other parts of the world.

1964 THE CLASSIC COMEDY SERIES Bewitched is first screened on US TV. It is subsequently shown in many different countries all over the world.

976 THE WORLD HEALTH Organization recommends that witch doctors join medical teams in Africa.

African shaman performing a healing ritual

1996–1999

1996 THE POPULAR TV COMEDY, Sabrina the Teenage Witch, is first screened on US TV.

1997 J.K. ROWLING publishes the first of the Harry Potter series of books, Harry Potter and the Philosopher's Stone. The book becomes a worldwide phenomenal success.

1999 THE BLAIR WITCH PROJECT becomes the most profitable film ever made. The fascination with witches is stronger than ever.

the pentagram—a magic symbol

2000–

2000 J.K. ROWLING publishes the fourth in the Harry Potter series of books, Harry Potter and the Goblet of Fire. It becomes one of the most successful books ever.

SHAMANISM is still practiced in many places around the world, such as Nepal, Indonesia, and Aboriginal Australia.

Aboriginal shaman

GLOSSARY

alchemy
The art of trying to turn base (ordinary) metals, such as lead, into precious ones, such as silver or gold. Alchemists also tried to find the secret of everlasting life.

amulet
An object believed to have magical properties and the ability to protect someone or something against evil.

astrology
The art of studying the stars and planets to foretell the future.

black magic
The art of causing harm through magic.

Catholic Church
A branch of the Christian Church, governed by the Pope in Rome.

cauldron
A large metal pot, supposedly used by witches to brew their spells. A symbol of female energy in modern witchcraft.

charm
An object or a saying believed to have magical powers.

Christianity
The belief that there is one god, whose son Jesus Christ came to Earth to save humankind.

curse
A magical act performed in order to harm or trouble someone.

demon
An evil spirit.

Devil
The most evil being, and enemy of God. Also known as Satan.

Devil's Marks
Marks on the body, such as scars or moles, said to have been put there by the Devil to identify his followers.

divination
Foretelling the future.

Early Modern
The period in European history between 1450 and 1650. It followed the Medieval period, and was the time when witch-hunting began.

elixir of life
A substance sought by alchemists that would give them the secret of eternal life. See also philosopher's stone.

familiar
A spirit that serves a witch, which appears in the shape of an animal, such as a toad.

Halloween
A Christian festival held on October 31st, which replaces the old European festival Samhain. It gets its name from All Hallows (All Saints) Eve, which takes place on November 1st.

heretic
One who practices a heresy—a religious teaching that does not follow the authorized teaching of the Church.

hex doll
A doll used in witchcraft to place a curse or put a spell on a person. Also called a poppet.

Inquisition
A court of the Catholic Church, set up in 1233, which was responsible for finding heretics and punishing them.

magic
The art of contacting a spirit world.

magician
Someone who practices magic.

mandrake
A plant thought to have magical powers, the root of which looks like a human being.

medicine man or woman
A member of a tribe who heals and helps people through the use of magical rituals. See also witch doctor.

Medieval
A term describing people, events, or objects of the Middle Ages.

medium
A person who is thought to have the ability to communicate with the dead.

Middle Ages
The period in European history between 1050 and 1450.

occult
Anything that involves magical, hidden forces.

oracle
In ancient Greece or Rome, a priest or a priestess through whom the gods were believed to speak and to foretell the future.

pagan
Someone or something that relates to ancient religions, in which many gods are worshipped.

persecution
The act of finding and punishing members of a certain section of society because of their beliefs, their identity, or their actions.

philosopher's stone
A substance sought by alchemists that would help them to turn base (ordinary) metals into gold. See also elixir of life.

propaganda
Information distributed with the intentional aim of influencing peoples' opinions.

Protestant Church
Any of the branches of the Christian Church that separated themselves from the Catholic Church in the 1500s, during the period called the Reformation.

ritual
Traditional words and actions that are repeated every time a certain ceremony takes place.

Roman Empire
Large parts of Europe, Africa, and Asia, ruled by the Romans between 27 B.C. and A.D. 476.

sabbat
A ceremony in which witches were said to worship the Devil and perform evil acts.

Satanism
Devil worship.

scrying
Foretelling the future.

shaman
A member of a tribe who uses magic to heal and help people.

shape-shifting
The art of changing shape, supposed to have been one of the skills of a witch.

sorcerer
Someone who practices magic.

spell
A set of magic words and actions that can be used to influence people and events.

spirit
A being from another realm, either an ancestor or a plant or animal helper.

spiritualism
The practice of talking to the spirit world through a medium.

Stone Age
The period in human history when tools and weapons were made of stone.

supernatural
Any event or occurrence that cannot be explained by science.

tarot cards
A pack of 78 cards designed to tell the future. The first known reference to them comes from the Middle Ages.

trance
A sleep-like state where some communicate with the spirits.

trial
A gathering in which a person accused of a crime is found innocent or guilty, depending on the evidence given.

trick or treat
A recent Halloween tradition, in which children ask for candy or small gifts in return for not playing a naughty trick.

warlock
A male witch.

Wicca
A modern, nature-worshipping religion.

wise man or woman
A person who traditionally used magic to heal and help people. Also called cunning folk.

witch
Someone, usually a woman, who possesses magical powers and who practices witchcraft.

witch doctor
A man or woman in a tribe who uses magic to heal and help people. See also medicine man or woman.

witch-hunt
The act of finding witches in order to punish them.

witchcraft
The art of using magic.

wizard
A man who possesses magical powers.

INDEX